WITHDRAWN

D0054048

RENEWALS 458-4574
DATE DUE

JUL 1 0			
FEB - 2			
GAYLORD			PRINTED IN U.S.A.

THE
POLICE DETECTIVE
FUNCTION

THE
POLICE DETECTIVE
FUNCTION

By

V. A. LEONARD, B.S., M.S., Ph.D.

Professor Emeritus of Police Administration
Washington State University
Pullman, Washington

CHARLES C THOMAS • PUBLISHER

Springfield • Illinois • U.S.A.

Published and Distributed Throughout the World by
CHARLES C THOMAS • PUBLISHER
Bannerstone House
301-327 East Lawrence Avenue, Springfield, Illinois, U.S.A.
Natchez Plantation House
735 North Atlantic Boulevard, Fort Lauderdale, Florida, U.S.A.

This book is protected by copyright. No part of it
may be reproduced in any manner without written
permission from the publisher.

© 1970, by CHARLES C THOMAS • PUBLISHER

Library of Congress Catalog Card Number: 79-119981

With THOMAS BOOKS careful attention is given to all details of manufacturing and design. It is the Publisher's desire to present books that are satisfactory as to their physical qualities and artistic possibilities and appropriate for their particular use. THOMAS BOOKS will be true to those laws of quality that assure a good name and good will.

Printed in the United States of America
RV-1

LIBRARY
University of Texas
At San Antonio

PREFACE

MOST of the texts and reference works in police literature are addressed to the problems of the larger police department. *The Police Detective Function* has been written specifically for the more than 33,000 smaller departments of the nation, with a personnel strength of from one to seventy-five officers — where a large segment of police service in this country is delivered.

Structuring the detective function in police organization is a basic administrative problem that confronts every department. It must be located in the organizational structure where the investigative process will be favored with the maximum use of personnel resources at the disposal of the organization.

Freeways, main arterials and other features of a modern highway system, together with the mobility of the criminal population today, mean simply that the exposure of the smaller community to criminal attack has increased on a disturbing scale. A high premium is thus placed upon the efficiency with which the detective function is discharged.

Criminal investigation involves the detection and apprehension of the criminal offender and the production of evidence against him. It is the point at which society brings the forces of law and order into sharp focus in its approach to the problems of crime and the criminal. In order to structure the detective function under sound principles of organization and management, it is first necessary to review the commanding role of patrol service in a police organization.

Numerically, it is at once, and should be, the largest single unit in both the staff and line of a police department. The patrol force marks the point in police organization where planning, strategy and policy are translated into action in the field, in the approach to the major objectives of police service. These include the protection of life and property, prevention and suppression of crime and vice, apprehension of criminal offenders, recovery of lost and stolen property, preservation of the public peace and order, and the regulation and control of traffic.

All other line units in a police organization move in orbit about the patrol force *and are secondary to it.* This basic principle of organization is of the utmost importance to the smaller department where success in the delivery of police service is dependent upon a relatively small number of officers.

Since the work of the patrol force includes all major police functions, the more effective patrol service is, the less need there will be for the more specialized operating units.

It is fundamental that tasks ordinarily assumed by specialized units and divisions that can be satisfactorily performed by the patrol force should be reserved for the patrol so that its manpower may be increased and the personnel strength of the special unit decreased or eliminated altogether. In cities and communities of 100,000 and under, perhaps even higher, the presence of a detective unit or division would seem to be a waste of departmental resources. In such jurisdictions, there appears to be no sound reason for not locating total investigative responsibility in the patrol force.

A compelling prerequisite for the elimination of this special deployment of patrol personnel resources is a determination of policy by police management with respect to *patrol beat responsibility.* Everything pivots on this determination. The trend, especially in the smaller department, is toward the "generalist" or all-purpose patrolman, where total case investigation and case clearance responsibilities are assigned to the officer on the beat. Under this administrative policy, he is completely responsible for the investigation and final disposition of all cases originating in the patrol area to which he is assigned.

As an example, the Police Department of Port Arthur, Texas, a town with a population of 66,676, has abolished the position of detective. The responsibility for all criminal investigation has been assigned to the patrol force. Structuring the detective function within the patrol services is the central thesis of Chapter I.

Locating the detective function exclusively with the patrol

force places a high premium on the quality of police personnel. It calls for a superior man in police uniform, superior recruiting standards and a superior training program, together with a salary structure that will attract this calibre of personnel. Chapter II examines police entrance qualifications, the residence requirement, the search for candidates, coordinated statewide recruiting, the police salary structure, in-service training and regional police training schools.

Attention is directed toward the significance of legislation at the state level prescribing minimum selection and training standards for entry into police service and the appearance of state commissions to implement this important legislation. In this chapter also, emphasis is placed upon the rapid advance of professional police training at the university and college level. It is now evident that the personnel resources of police organization and management are moving into a new era of capability and performance, with all this implied in terms of discharging the detective function within the patrol services. It means simply that the potential and capability are there to accommodate investigative responsibility and that this will be increasingly so in the days ahead.

Chapter III is concerned with the investigative process and the exposure of a police officer to investigative responsibility on three distinct fronts. The nature of the investigative process is considered, together with the equipment at the disposal of the investigating officer. In this connection, an inventory is presented of sources of information that are presently available to the investigator.

In Chapter IV, "The Care and Preservation of Evidence," the nature and classification of evidence are considered, along with the evidence resources of the crime scene and the necessity for a systematic and painstaking search of the area, particularly in crimes of stealth and violence. The care that must be taken in the preparation of the various types of evidence for transfer to police headquarters or to a nearby crime detection laboratory is emphasized. In the smaller department, it is noted that at least a rudimentary laboratory facility, including a photographic darkroom, merits a high priority.

Collateral elements of the investigative process are presented in Chapter V, including *modus operandi* as an important tool of criminal investigation, and the interrogation of witnesses and criminal suspects. The restrictions that have been imposed by the United States Supreme Court upon the police interrogation of a criminal suspect in the case of *Miranda v. Arizona* are carefully noted. The police use of the polygraph as an aid to interrogation is given detailed treatment. Appropriate attention is directed toward the important subject of investigation records and report writing.

The Police Detective Function has been written as a manual and convenient reference work for the chief and his officers in small and medium-sized police departments. In addition, it should prove useful as a training tool in local police training programs and in regional in-service training schools, as well as at the university and college level. The individual police officer may find it to be a useful addition to his personal library as a source of reference and study in his preparation for advancement in this professional field.

Additional books written by the author expressly for the smaller police department and available through the same publisher, include:

The Police Enterprise — Its Organization and Management
Police Personnel Management
The Police Records System
The Police Communications System
Police Patrol Organization

V. A. L.

CONTENTS

THE
POLICE DETECTIVE
FUNCTION

By the same author:
Police Communication Systems
Survey and Reorganization of the Seattle Police
Department
Police Organization and Management (First and
Second Editions)
A Guide to the Study of Police Organization and
Management
The Police of the 20th Century
The General Administration of Criminal Justice
(co-author)
Police Science for the Young American
The Police, the Judiciary and the Criminal
The Police Enterprise — Its Organization and
Management
Police Personnel Administration
The Police Records System
The Police Communications System
Police Patrol Organization

I

STRUCTURING THE DETECTIVE FUNCTION

THE DETECTIVE FUNCTION IN MODERN POLICE SERVICE

CRIMINAL INVESTIGATION is the keystone of police service. The detection and apprehension of the criminal offender and the production of evidence against him all depend upon it. It is the point at which society brings the forces of law and order into sharp focus in its approach to the problem of crime and the criminal. The detective function — *criminal investigation* — is a basic feature of modern police service.

Looking back through the pages of history, close surveillance and other basic investigative techniques are doubtless as old as the human race. However, it is believed that the detective function, as it is generally understood today, first appeared during the sixteenth and seventeenth centuries in England and France. In a period of rapidly increasing wealth, together with weak and corrupt governmental controls, the extent of robbery, burglary and other forms of crime became a matter of major official concern. Magistrates charged with the suppression of crime recognized the need for advance information concerning the activity of criminal offenders. The circumstances suggested the advantage of buying information from informers who themselves lived outside the pale of the law. On occasion, they were even engaged in the investigation of criminal cases.

COMMANDING ROLE OF PATROL SERVICE

Today, the role of the detective operation includes the primary objectives of apprehending those offenders who escape arrest at the hands of patrol service and recovering stolen property. In order to structure the detective function under sound principles of

3

organization and management, it is first necessary to review the commanding role of patrol service in a police organization.

Numerically, it is at once, and should be, the largest single unit in both the staff and line of a police department. In terms of work and performance, it carries out in police service the functions discharged by the combat elements in military operations. The patrol force marks the point in police organization where planning, strategy and policy are translated into action in the field, in the approach to the major objectives of police service:

1. Protection of life and property.
2. Prevention and suppression of crime and vice.
3. Apprehension of criminal offenders.
4. Recovery of lost and stolen property.
5. Preservation of the public peace and order.
6. Regulation and control of traffic.

All other line units in a police organization move in orbit about the patrol force and are *secondary to it.* This basic principle of organization is of the utmost importance to the smaller department where success in the delivery of police service is dependent upon a relatively small number of officers. Here, all the tools of management should be directed toward increasing the line power of the patrol force. Any organizational function or activity which does not serve this end and purpose represents lost motion and should be abandoned forthwith as a matter of sound administrative policy.

INROADS OF SPECIALIZATION

Since the work of the patrol force includes all major police functions, the more effective patrol service is, the less need there will be for the more specialized operating units. It may be impossible for the patrol force to be 100 per cent effective in the discharge of all police functions, but the other operating line units are necessary only to the extent that patrol service falls short of this ideal. It follows, therefore, that any attempt to create, improve or strengthen other units or divisions at the expense of the patrol force serves to pyramid the case load not only for the unit that has prospered through personnel transfers but for all other units and divisions in the department.

It is for this reason that any plans for the creation of special assignments, special details and new operating units in either the staff or line must be viewed with a strong mixture of candor and caution, especially in the smaller department. Specialization has made serious inroads upon the line power of the patrol force in American police department. Admittedly, as a department grows, some degree of specialization is necessary and desirable. However, heavy emphasis must be placed on eliminating, as far as possible, the sacrifice of front-line patrol forces in order to strengthen the shift toward specialization. The combat strength or striking power of the patrol force must be amplified at every possible opportunity. The following two examples illustrate the way in which this can be done.

The Traffic Control Function

In the growth of a police department and the expansion of its activities, the first major appearance of specialization usually occurs in the area of traffic regulation and control. Thus, it may become apparent to the chief and his command personnel that the increased demand on the patrolman's time in the investigation of traffic accidents and the need for increased skill in both traffic accident investigation and the enforcement of traffic laws indicate the need for the special assignment of an officer for the discharge of these functions.

Subsequently, a decision is made for the addition of another traffic officer and then another. With this increase in personnel assigned exclusively to the traffice function, the problem of supervision arises and a traffic unit is created. •

Then within the traffic unit, further specialization appears in the form of officers assigned exclusively to the enforcement of traffic laws and others to traffic accident investigation, where they are equipped with cameras and other instrumental aids for this type of investigation. There follow in turn specialists in the attack upon problems of pedestrian and street intersection control, together with a special statistical unit to expedite plans for selective enforcement operations, and traffic surveys and analyses.

Practically all of these new specialized assignments call for transfers of personnel from the patrol force, with a corresponding depletion of police line power in the field. It is important, therefore, to establish some criteria as a basis for determining the personnel strength of the traffic unit, or for that matter, for determining whether personnel should be assigned exclusively to the traffic function at all.

With the increasing interest, both nationally and locally, in the traffic problem, a tendency is observable in many jurisdictions to overemphasize the traffic unit or division and to misinterpret its role in police organization. In no small number of instances, police departments have become traffic-centered, with the result that unpardonable transfers of personnel have been made from the patrol force in order to raise the strength of the traffic unit or division up to standard.

In fact, it has become traditional practice to approach the traffic problem by building up expensive traffic divisions. There are those who hold that, based upon property losses, insurance rates and similar criteria, 25 percent of the total police problem is traffic in nature and that a corresponding percentage of the department's personnel and material resources should be assigned to the traffic function. It would be extremely hazardous to conclude that one-sixth, one-fourth or one-third of the total police problem was traffic in nature, for the reason that there are few instances indeed where anyone is actually in a position to know the true dimensions of crime and vice in the community.

Even if it were possible to assume that 25 percent of the total police problem in a given community or city could be accounted for by traffic accidents, parking, congestion, traffic flow and so forth, it would still be an erroneous and ill-conceived policy to assign 25 percent of departmental resources to the traffic function. Furthermore, it is a costly administrative mistake to assign to any one unit or division exclusive responsibility for meeting this important problem. It is more than a question of arithmetic. The traffic problem is too great for any one unit or division to cope with alone. Sound administrative practice dictates that the total line resources of the department, including primarily the patrol force, must be made available for meeting the problem when and where the records indicate this is necessary.

It is important to observe that there is nothing particularly occult about the investigation of a traffic accident. Given the intelligence and training, it matters little for the end result of a traffic accident investigation whether the patrolman is in a special accident-investigation car at the time of the emergency call or in a patrol car on his beat. The same considerations apply with equal emphasis to traffic-law enforcement. Thus, through eliminating the special assignment of officers to the traffic function, the strength of the patrol force is protected; and in bringing more power to bear upon the problem, the overall performance record of the department is enhanced.

A second example of unnecessary specialization involves the creation of the position of detective. In the smaller departments with a personnel strength up to seventy-five officers or more, this administrative error can be easily avoided.

The Detective Unit

As previously noted, the primary functions of the detective are to apprehend those offenders who escape arrest at the hands of the patrol force and to recover stolen property. In the growth of a police department, the necessity may eventually arise for the creation of the position of detective when the uncleared case load of the patrol force reaches a point where departmental efficiency indicates the need for specialized assistance. The number of these offenses and the grave character of many of them may, in the course of time, make necessary the organization of a separate unit in the department manned by persons assigned exclusively to criminal investigation.

In the larger cities, as the department grows and the case load expands, specialization develops within the detective unit or division itself. Such specialization permits the investigator to concentrate his time and energies in the investigation of a particular type of criminal activity. Through continuous work in a specific criminal area, he gradually builds up a fund of skills and information which contributes to departmental efficiency and performance. He comes to know personally the offenders who operate within the specific criminal specialty; he becomes familiar with their methods of operation or *modus operandi*, their habits, friends, relatives and close associates. Not infrequently, an experienced detective is able to narrow the investigation and search down to a single individual after a careful study of the crime scene and recognition of the salient features of the *modus operandi.*

As a result of the yield from specialization in criminal investigation, detective divisions, particularly in the larger cities, are decentralized functionally into special details such as the homicide, robbery, burglary, automobile theft, worthless check, bunco and other specialized squads. Case-load volume usually determines the necessity for the creation of a specialized squad. Such units should be created only in response to a real need and liquidated or consolidated with another unit when the need has passed or ceased to be acute or continuous.

Here again, detective units are manned by transfers from the patrol force, the backbone of a police organization, with a corresponding depletion in the line power of this basic unit of police service. There are important alternatives to the conventional detective, particularly in the smaller departments with a personnel strength up to seventy-five officers or more.

It is fundamental that tasks ordinarily assumed by specialized units and divisions that can be satisfactorily performed by the patrol force should be reserved for the patrol so that its manpower may be increased and the personnel strength of the special unit decreased or eliminated altogether. In cities and communities of 150,000 population and under, perhaps even higher, the presence of a detective unit or division would seem to be a waste of departmental resources. In such jurisdictions, there appears to be no sound reason for not locating total investigative responsibility in the patrol force.

In those instances where the individual patrolman is in need of specialized investigative assistance or where the investigation might take him beyond the boundaries of his beat, experienced patrolmen operating in plain clothes, if necessary, and under the control of the patrol commander, should be able to perform this service effectively. Patrolmen can be selected for this assignment on the basis of demonstrated aptitudes and capabilities for the different types of case investigations.

In addition to the economy in money and manpower, this arrangement would eliminate split-division responsibility for case investigation, with the added advantage of concentrating the total investigative function under the control of one man — the patrol commander. In at least one known instance, this improvement has been made; there are undoubtedly others. The police department of Port Arthur, Texas, a town with a population of 66,676, has abolished the position of detective. The responsibility for all criminal investigation has been assigned to the patrol force.

PATROL BEAT RESPONSIBILITY

The foregoing two examples of unnecessary specialization, with their unfortunate depletion of patrol power, apply with equal force to all other assignments to special details and special operating units. The compelling requirement or prerequisite for the elimination of this special deployment of patrol personnel resources is a determination of policy by police management with respect to *patrol beat responsibility.* Everything pivots on this determination.

Policy in regard to this critical decision, which is among the gravest problems presented to police administration, will vary from one department to another. At one end of the administrative spectrum, the detective is charged with total investigative responsibility. The patrolman merely responds to the radio call, makes an arrest if perchance this is possible and protects the crime scene until the detectives arrive to launch the investigation.

Under this ill-advised policy, the detective unit usually finds itself overloaded with uncleared cases in every crime category, with the result that major crime fails to receive the attention that it deserves, and the patrolman has relatively little to do. It is difficult to escape the observation that under this arrangement, the department experiences a tragic waste of manpower because of the unused resources of the patrol force — this despite the sobering fact that patrol salaries represent the largest single item in the total police budget.

There follow in succession those departments where the patrol officer is held responsible for the preliminary investigation of cases originating on his beat and the filing of a report covering his investigative activities on the case. The follow-up investigation and final clearance of the case are a responsibility of the detective, except perhaps in a few minor cases.

At the other end of the spectrum is the department operating under a policy where virtually all total case investigation and case-clearance responsibility are assigned to the officer on the beat. Under this administrative concept, the officer is responsible for the investigation and clearance of all cases originating on his beat, regardless of classification.

He is geared to the total delivery of police service, which means that he is held responsible for the robbery rate, the burglary rate, the automobile theft rate, the amount of larceny, the extent of juvenile delinquency, the number of traffic accidents, the amount of traffic congestion, and all other police problems that originate within the limits of the patrol area to which he is assigned. All uncleared cases represent a direct charge against the efficiency of the individual patrolman concerned and provide a fair index to his general performance record. Referred to by some as the "all-purpose patrolman" and by Bristow as "the Generalist,"* he is totally responsible for the case investigation and its final disposition in all categories.

The following significant paragraph appears in the general information bulletin for applicants furnished by one police department to potential candidates for the position of patrolman, before an application form is issued:

> A patrolman is responsible for all crimes or reports arising on his beat. The officer reports off his beat after completing his tour of duty and is then required to write reports on all cases handled by him. This may take only a few minutes or it may take several hours, depending upon the nature of the reports handled and the ability of the individual. Patrolmen are held responsible for the investigation of all complaints regardless of seriousness and regardless of the fact that detectives or supervisory officers may assist and counsel in the investigation.

---

*Bristow, Allen P.: *Effective Police Manpower Utilization.* Springfield, Thomas, 1969, p. 18.

Obviously, the individual officer cannot discharge all of these duties and responsibilities without considerable assistance from others, and for this reason, he has at his disposal the entire resources of the department. The facilities of the detective unit, or in any jurisdiction where the position of detective has been abolished, experienced patrolmen in plain clothes, are available to give the necessary assistance in the investigation of felony cases, and in other instances where the case investigation would take the officer beyond the boundaries of his beat.

Members of the crime-prevention unit likewise come to his assistance in the solution of problems associated with the prevalence of juvenile delinquency in the area to which he is assigned. Similarly, the facilities of the crime laboratory, whether it is a local, state or national facility, the records unit, the vice officer or officers and all other administrative units in the organization cooperate with the individual patrolman in keeping his beat clean.

But regardless of the type or volume of assistance the officer may bring into play, he cannot pass the buck; the responsibility for the delivery of police service in that area to which he is assigned belongs exclusively to him. Such a system requires a superior man in police uniform, superior recruiting standards and a superior training program, together with a salary structure that will attract this type of personnel*. Today, this is the calibre of manpower that is being recruited on an increasing scale into the American police services.

THE FLUID PATROL SYSTEM

The fluid patrol system concept, now attracting wide attention in police circles, offers still more cogent reasons for structuring the detective function within the patrol services. Originating with the Aberdeen plan and later the Salford plan, in England, the implementation of the fluid patrol system operation in the United States has led the police to combine some of the features of these two plans with the tactical unit or mobile task force concept.

*Leonard, V. A.: *Police Personnel Management.* Springfield, Thomas, 1970.

Probably the most notable application of the fluid patrol system is in the police department of Tucson, Arizona, where it was placed in operation in 1963. As of 1965, the thirty patrol beats covering an area of 72 square miles were abolished and replaced with the new patrol system.

The city is divided into small grids or reporting districts of approximately one-quarter square mile in area. Crime data and data concerning other demands for police service are tabulated by grids, from which special reports are prepared by the police records unit and made available to the patrol commander at the beginning of each tour of duty. The platoon is divided into squads, each under the command of a field sergeant.

The city was separated into four subsectors, with a sergeant and his squad assigned to each subsector. The sergeant is held responsible for squad operations. He may require one or two of his six or seven officers to report for duty in plain clothes for a stake-out or other assignment; he may assign two or more officers to patrol the entire subsector; he may keep two or more officers with him for saturation patrol of two or more "hot" grids – all depending on the flow of reports from the police records unit and what they have to say about the current situation.

Under certain emergency conditions, the radio dispatcher may direct all broadcasts to the sergeant, and he in turn assigns his men accordingly. This arrangement represents a special type of de-centralization in which for the duration of the emergency, radio control is temporarily vested in the field, subject, of course, to the receipt of additional instructions and information from head-quarters. From the standpoint of police records administration and investigative responsibility, when a member of a squad becomes involved in a case investigation, he carries it through to final disposition. As an alternative, one or more officers may be assigned exclusively to follow up case investigation.

The Police Department of Oakland, California, among others, is considering the installation of the fluid patrol system. They contemplate the possibility of hourly reports from the police records division, making possible the shifting of patrol personnel hour by hour into sections of the community where and when current records data indicate the greatest demand for police service is most likely to occur.

The police records unit is the lifeblood of the fluid patrol system. The mainstay of the system in Tucson is the computer and machine tabulation of statistical data based upon the grid or reporting area.

It is here strongly recommended that departments with a personnel strength up to seventy-five officers or more make a conversion to the grid system of reporting and tabulating criminal offenses, traffic accidents and other calls for police service. In the smaller departments where a computer installation would be impractical, the manual processing of records data presents no problem.

Whether the department moves toward the fluid system of patrol deployment or remains with the conventional patrol beat concept, the grid system of reporting will expedite a sound determination of patrol areas based upon the crime and traffic accident experience. It is further recommended that all departments begin experimenting with the fluid patrol concept. This may well prove to be one of the major disappointments of the present era for the criminal offender.

In that connection, two books are recommended for every departmental library: *Effective Police Manpower Utilization,* by Allen P. Bristow, Charles C Thomas, Publisher, Springfield, Illinois; and *Police Patrol Readings,* by Samuel G. Chapman, by the same publisher.

It can be readily seen that the fluid patrol system offers an ideal framework in which to structure the detective function within the patrol services.

II

PERSONNEL REQUIREMENTS

STRUCTURING the detective function within the patrol services places a high premium on the quality of police personnel. It has been previously indicated that the system requires a superior man in police uniform, superior recruiting standards and a superior training program, together with a salary structure that will attract this calibre of personnel. It is patent that the detective function must be discharged by a trained and experienced police officer with demonstrated skills and aptitudes in the techniques of criminal investigation.

The personnel resources of a police department are its greatest asset, and this is particularly true of the detective function. All the way from the top to the bottom of the enterprise, the quality of personnel sets the stage for standards of performance in the delivery of police service. Furthermore, the degree of intelligence, zeal, determination and devotion to duty that a police officer brings to roll call as he prepares for his tour of duty is determined in advance by recruiting standards at the intake.

Fundamental to successful police service in the small and medium-sized community is the individual police officer, selected with care and well-trained for the job. The patrolman of today is the sergeant, the lieutenant, the captain, the chief of police of tomorrow. Thus, the character of police service for years to come is almost completely determined by personnel policy and, very largely at the intake, by recruiting standards. Police chiefs and other officials of local government are recognizing this basic principle, and as a result, recruiting standards are moving upward in order to attract to police service career-minded young men and women.

ENTRANCE STANDARDS FOR POLICE SERVICE

Police entrance qualifications must be geared to the demands of the detective function. Criminal investigation requires a superior calibre of personnel. All the way from age, height, intelligence, educational background, robust physical and mental health to emotional stability and character that is unassailable, the man in uniform or in plain clothes must be a high grade of human material.

In regard to the age requirement, there has been an observable trend toward a reduction in age limits. The police are realizing that the younger man is more flexible and more easy to mold to the aims, ideals and standards of the department. They learn easier and faster in the police training school. They possess more vigor, energy and alertness than the older man and are not likely to have their initiative stifled by some previous job failure. The career-minded man is the young man.

Today, the age of twenty-one is widely considered as the absolute minimum limit for entry into police service. There is strong testimony for fixing the maximum age limit no higher than twenty-five, and there is strong evidence to indicate that men between the age limits of twenty-one and twenty-five make the best material for policemen.

An examination of entrance qualification schedules in American police departments reveals a height range from five feet, five inches, to six feet, six inches. The small man is invaluable at times in police service, but there is a psychological advantage that goes with the larger man in the control of people singly or in groups that is generally not overlooked. Most departments have arrived at the average of five feet, ten inches.

Where formerly two hundred pounds of brawn constituted the primary requirement for service in a police uniform, the weight factor now possesses only a nominal significance. The requirement will vary from one jurisdiction to another, but most departments agree upon a minimum of 150 pounds. A reasonable and safe procedure is to consider weight in proportion to height.

The candidate must possess robust physical health in every respect, as determined by a competent doctor of medicine. Equally important, reliable determinations must be made with respect to mental health, personality, nervous condition, temperament, social intellect, habits and ideals. The services of a psychiatrist in making these evaluations are usually available nearby.

A candidate who is in doubtful health should be rejected. In addition to the liability of substandard performance, he may become a pensioner in a short time with the necessity of replacing him, and with the result that two men are carried on the payroll for the rest of their lives rather than one. Days lost on account of sickness in American police departments continue as a serious drain on the effective personnel strength of the department and add tremendously to the cost of police protection in this country.

The same considerations which dictate a rigid physical examination for all candidates suggest the necessity of annual physical examinations for all departmental personnel. From the standpoint of preventive medicine, incipient difficulties may be discovered and proper remedial measures taken at a time when they can produce the best results. Such examinations serve the interests of both the officer and the department, particularly in the small and medium-sized communities.

Both physical strength and agility should be required of the police applicant to a superior degree. Appropriate tests designed to measure these qualities may be obtained from the Department of Physical Education at any nearby college or university.

It is extremely doubtful that there ever was a *successful* police officer who was not unusually intelligent. The highest degree of intelligence available is none too good for the trying tasks that daily confront a police officer. The organizational chain is no stronger than its weakest link, and the stupid, blundering individual, who by his acts can bring discredit upon an entire organization, becomes the public's measuring stick for the whole department. One inferior man who fails to rise to an emergency can prejudice the reputation of an otherwise excellent police force.

Rapid and accurate thinking is an essential quality of the police officer. He must reach decisions concerning the application of the law without delay. An officer's perceptive powers, his imagination, his ability to concentrate his attention upon the tasks that are before him, his memory — visual and auditory — and his reasoning and judgment must all be of the best. Otherwise, the individual must fail when confronted with some of the crucial tests that are the lot of every police officer.

Educational requirements in American police departments vary from the ability to read and write to high school graduation, with the trend definitely toward the requirement of a university degree in police science and administration. In terms of aptitudes, exceptional personal qualities *are necessary* for the satisfactory performance of police duty.* Many of them are quite fundamental to the successful discharge of the detective function and should be present to a degree beyond that of the average individual.

The character and reputation of a police officer must be unassailable. Police entrance examination procedure must include a state and national fingerprint clearance and a thorough background investigation. The application form filled in by the police candidate should be of such a nature that it will furnish a wide range of investigative leads.

One of the most disabling obstacles to career service in the police field is the "home talent" tradition still prevailing in too many American cities and communities. This expresses itself in the local residence requirement for appointment to the force. In order that patrol service in general and the detective function in particular may have the highest calibre of personnel, the police and other officials of local government should take immediate steps to abolish the local residence requirement and also state residence requirements, if they exist. It is noteworthy that in recent years, an increasing number of communities have abandoned the residence qualification and require only that the candidate be a citizen of the United States.

THE SEARCH FOR CANDIDATES

Following the establishment of adequate entrance standards, the next and perhaps the most essential phase of the whole recruitment process is an active search for candidates. Where the residence requirement has been disposed of, this can cover a comparatively wide area. Police departments and police

---

*Leonard, V. A.: *Police Personnel Administration.* Springfield, Thomas, 1969.

associations in each state should take the initiative and pool their resources in the establishment of a coordinated statewide program of recruiting candidates. This would be especially helpful to the smaller departments, where the field of potential candidates is limited. In those states where state commissions on minimum selection and training standards have been established, the commission is in an excellent position to organize and administer a coordinated statewide recruiting program.

THE EXAMINATION PROCESS

Basic to the screening process is the written examination. The intelligent use of tests and examinations, now accepted as standard procedure in the best American police departments, will go far toward reducing the element of chance in the selection of police personnel. Contact with the police personnel officer in nearby cities and the state police will prove fruitful in connection with the selection of tests and the content of the written examination. It should include at least one recognized intelligence test such as the Army Alpha, the Otis Self-Administering Test or the Henmon-Nelson Test of Mental Ability.

A probationary period of not less than one year, preferably two, is an indispensable feature of the examination process. During this period, superior officers may give close attention to the candidate's actual ability to do police work before tenure protection becomes absolute. No probationer should be given tenure until the end of the probationary period and only then upon the specific recommendation of his superiors. The department should be given the benefit of the doubt in all borderline cases.

Some form of rating system by which superior officers may at regular intervals appraise the desirable and undesirable qualities of the new recruit is a necessary and important phase of personnel management. Rating procedure thus becomes integrated with the probationary period as a continuing part of the screening process. Those individuals who cannot or do not measure up to departmental standards of performance need to be eliminated at as early a stage as possible. Effective rating forms, together with instructions for their use, would be obtainable from the personnel officer of police departments in nearby cities, or from the United States Civil Service Commission in Washington, D. C.

POLICE SALARY STRUCTURE

The calibre of police personnel carries with it important implications in terms of the police salary structure. In recent years, police salaries have moved generally upward. However, one of the difficulties in the past and in the present has been a widespread tendency to handcuff police salaries to salary levels prevailing in fire departments. This unfortunate combination is based upon the illusion that police and fire protection are of much the same nature. As a matter of fact, the day-to-day problems of the two departments have little in common. The police deal almost wholly with human relations while the work of the fireman is largely concerned with physical property.

All of the foregoing considerations pose important implications for the police in the smaller communities of the nation. Freeways, main arterials and other features of a modern highway system, together with the mobility of the criminal population today, mean simply that the exposure of the smaller community to criminal attack has increased on a disturbing scale. This, together with the growing complexity of the traffic problem, places a high premium on the quality of police performance in these communities.

The officials of local government would do well to reexamine their thinking in this respect with the view of adjusting police salaries upward to the point where they will be consistent with the quality and quantity of work to be done. Mounting crime rates, together with the growing demands of traffic control, are grounds for sober reflection on the part of these officials. They are under obligation to the community and its security to see to it, as the first order of business, that the personnel resources of the police are equal to the demands of a modern, complex social order.

TRAINING PROGRAM

Even after police recruits are selected by the best methods

available, the police structure will continue to remain unsound as long as it is generally assumed that a person with any type of training, or with none at all, is qualified to perform police duties. Where the nature and potentials of patrol service are properly understood by police management, it will be readily recognized that the technical aspects of every phase of patrol operations require training of a high order.

The whole matter assumes overwhelming importance when the technical requirements of criminal investigation are taken into account. It is significant to note that the exposure of the patrol officer to investigative responsibility occurs on three fronts:

1. In those departments where the patrolman is responsible for the total delivery of police service, including the clearance and disposition of all cases originating on his beat, criminal investigation is an integral part of the day's work.
2. Where the case load of the patrol force or other circumstances dictates the use of a patrolman or patrolmen in plain clothes, the day or night is devoted exclusively to criminal investigation. In both 1 and 2, the detective function is structured within the patrol services.
3. It has been previously noted that in the larger cities, it is routine procedure among police departments to recruit detectives from members of the patrol force. Here again, the undivided time and energies of the officer, now a detective, are spent in the investigation of criminal cases.

Thus, an in-service training facility, staffed by the most competent officers available and operating continuously the year around, must be brought to the doorstep of every police officer in every department. Especially is this true in view of the fact that for some time to come, the police recruit must be accepted in the raw, unprepared for the rigorous and exacting responsibilities of patrol service. Unlike workers in health, engineering and the other professions, he must be trained on the job at public expense.

In 1965, a survey of 1,352 cities conducted by the International City Managers' Association, revealed that 1,135 police departments were operating some type of in-service training program for their officers.

A recent survey of 269 departments by the National League of

Cities, conducted in 1966, reported that 97 percent of the departments surveyed were engaged in formal in-service training. But another survey of 4,000 police departments by the International Association of Chiefs of Police revealed that 85 percent of the officers appointed were sent into the field prior to their recruit training.*

It is now widely accepted that the following course subjects should be included in a police recruit training program:

Required Courses

1. Classroom note taking.
2. The role of law enforcement.
3. Police community relations.
4. Police ethics.
5. Racial and minority groups.
6. Laws of arrest, search and seizure, and Constitutional guarantees.
7. Code of criminal procedure and criminal law.
8. Vehicle and traffic law.
9. Traffic regulation and control.
10. Traffic accident investigation.
11. Laws of evidence.
12. Evidence resources in a criminal case, including the crime-scene search.
13. Collection, care, identification and preservation of evidence.
14. Court organization and procedure.
15. Courtroom demeanor and testifying.
16. Basic criminal investigation.
17. Note taking and report writing.
18. Interviews, interrogation, admissions, statements.
19. The patrol function.
20. Care and use of firearms.
21. Defensive tactics.
22. Techniques and mechanics of arrest.

---

*The President's Commission on Law Enforcement and the Administration of Justice: *Task Force Report, The Police.* U. S. Government Printing Office, 1967, p. 138.

23. Emergency aid to persons.
24. Recognition and handling of abnormal persons.
25. Juvenile offender laws, Juvenile Court, handling of juveniles.
26. Crowd and riot control.
27. Use of police radio and teletype.

Elective Courses

1. Special investigative techniques – gambling, narcotics, prostitution.
2. Driver training.
3. Care and maintenance of police equipment.
4. Administration of criminal justice.
5. Fingerprint indentification.
6. Jail procedures.
7. Jurisdiction of other law enforcement agencies.
8. The police records system.
9. Powers and duties of the sheriff.
10. Raid techniques, stake-outs, surveillance.
11. Scientific aid – the crime laboratory.
12. Police-press relations.
13. Transportation of prisoners.

The facilities are potentially available for an effective in-service training program in this country, and the police field itself is in general agreement concerning the curriculum content of an in-service training program. The problem is how to organize it and bring it into contact with those who need the training.

This is particularly true of small and medium-sized police departments where in many instances, it would be impractical to organize and put into operation an in-service police training school. Authorities agree that it would be economically feasible to establish a departmental training school where the personnel strength was from fifteen to twenty officers or more, and that it would not be feasible to do so with a group of two or three officers.

The answers appear to be coming into focus and at an accelerated tempo during the past two decades. Over the years, metropolitan police departments have, on occasion, extended their training facilities to members of the smaller police forces in the surrounding suburban areas. Under this arrangement, selected officers attend the metropolitan school from communities within a radius of from fifty to one hundred miles.

The Federal Bureau of Investigation has for a number of years placed at the disposal of local law enforcement agencies the superb training facilities of that organization. Under the name of the National Police Academy, this program is available to selected officers from police departments in every part of the United States. The Bureau has also conducted a series of regional law enforcement training programs in all of the states. Such training schools are usually scheduled at central points, and officers attend them from the surrounding area.

Some state police organizations have also made their training facilities available to local law enforcement agencies through the staging of regional training schools. The resources of the state have also been applied to police in-service training through other channels. Texas Agricultural and Mechanical University, Pennsylvania State University, Iowa State University, University of Oklahoma, Michigan State University, Indiana University and other educational institutions have made notable contributions in the organization of in-service training programs on a zone or regional basis.

But the American police services have now entered a new era in terms of their most vital resource — personnel. Escaping the attention of most observers, the time is now close at hand when the best in police practice and procedure will be brought to the doorstep of every police officer in the nation.

The new era finds expression on two major fronts — legislation at the state level prescribing minimum selection and training standards for entry into police service, and the emergence of professional police training curricula at the academic level in the universities and colleges of this country. Both developments sharpen the focus on the American police field as a career service and promise a new day for patrol service in every community.

The New York State Legislature in 1959 enacted into law the *Municipal Police Training Council Act,* which led to the adoption of an 80-hour minimum Basic Training Course, consisting of seventeen separate course subject areas. As of July 1, 1960, any one appointed as a police officer in that state is required to satisfactorily complete the basic course as a condition for permanent employment.

The first year of operation saw the completion of thirty-five basic schools of instruction throughout the state and the awarding of certificates to 822 police officers. It is significant that these 822 graduates are employed by 267 different municipalities within the state, indicating that the benefits of this police training program have been broadly dispersed throughout every area of New York State.

It will be noted that the minimum police training standards program in New York is mandatory. In other words, an applicant must complete satisfactorily a basic police training course before he can enter police service. It is *mandated* police training by state mandate.

Similar legislation was passed by the California State Legislature on October 23, 1960, establishing minimum police training standards for California police officers and providing for the certification of schools where this training may be obtained. The program is not mandatory; it is organized on a voluntary basis. It is significant to note that the individual applicant may substitute for the prescribed basic training course satisfactory completion of a minimum of sixty credit hours in an undergraduate police science major leading to a degree at any university or college certified by the State Training Commission.

Today in California, police training that meets the standards of the Commission is state-wide; it blankets the state and exceeds by far any to be found elsewhere in the nation, with the exception of the state of New York. In California by 1966, 98 percent of the population in that state was being served by police departments which adhered to the prescribed minimum standards for police training.

Legislation at the state level establishing minimum selection and training standards has also been enacted into law in New Jersey and Oregon, among others. By 1969, such legislation had been passed in a total of nine states. In a number of other states, similar legislation is under consideration. It is now evident that this development in the American police field marks a new milestone in police in-service training.

Apparently, it is just a matter of time until every state in the nation will have established minimum standards for the selection and training of police officers. This means that police practice and procedure in the training of police personnel is on the way toward making total contact with the field, including especially the smaller police departments of this country.

As an important step in this direction, in 1966, a Model Police Minimum Selection and Training Standards Council Act was drafted by the International Association of Chiefs of Police. It offers to the states a legislative model or pattern which can be followed in the establishment of minimum standards. for the selection and training of police personnel.

Police departments and state police associations in those states where such enabling legislation has not yet been passed should make strong and effective contact with the members of their legislatures and call their attention to these developments. Such action will accelerate the day when police personnel in all of the smaller police departments of the nation will have the benefit of adequate police selection and training facilities. It marks a new day for the patrol services.

Today, universities and colleges in this country are bringing their resources for training and research into contact with the personnel needs of the American police field. It is now possible for a high school graduate to prepare for a career in police service in the same manner as the doctor, lawyer and engineer. As of 1969, more than two hundred eighty-five universities and colleges in the United States were offering academic programs in preparation for career service in the police field.

Recently, the International Association of Chiefs of Police, with the aid of a $400,000 grant from the Ford Foundation, threw the full weight of its power and prestige behind police training at the university level. It can be expected with complete certainty that within a comparatively short time, university police training will blanket the nation, with a plurality of programs in every state.

Today, police recruiters are on the campuses of the nation

seeking out candidates for the entrance examination. Many police departments now offer extra credit on the entrance examination where the candidate possesses a degree in the police science major. An increasing number of departments have established a minimum educational requirement of two years of college work in police science and administration. In some departments already, the candidate must present a Bachelor's degree in the police science major in order to gain admission to the entrance examination room.

The foregoing pages demonstrate that the personnel resources of police organization and management are moving into a new era of capability and performance, with all this implies in terms of discharging the detective function within the patrol services. It all means simply that the potential and capability are there to accommodate investigative responsibility and that they will be increasingly so in the days ahead.

III

THE INVESTIGATIVE PROCESS

IF selected with care and adequately trained for police service, the individual patrol officer is in a strong position to undertake the responsibilities of case investigation. It is important to observe again that the exposure of the officer to investigative responsibility occurs on three fronts:
1. In those departments where the patrolman is held responsible for the total delivery of police service, including the clearance and disposition of all cases originating on his beat, criminal investigation is an integral part of the day's work.
2. Where the case load of the patrol force or other circumstances dictate the use of a patrolman, or patrolmen, in plain clothes, the day or night is devoted exclusively to criminal investigation. In both 1 and 2, the detective function is structured within the patrol services. Again in both 1 and 2, by the very nature of the task, the officer finds himself in a training environment which offers strong preparation for the discharge of the detective function.
3. It has been previously noted that in the larger cities, it is routine procedure among police departments to recruit detectives from members of the patrol force. Here again, the undivided time and energies of the officer are spent in the investigation of criminal cases.

NATURE OF THE INVESTIGATIVE PROCESS

Webster defines investigation as observing or studying by close examination and systematic inquiry. Criminal investigation involves four specific objectives:
1. *Establishing the fact that a criminal offense has been committed.* This is the *corpus delicti* or the body of the crime, which embraces all of the facts related to the

27

commission of a particular criminal offense and the fact that it was committed by a human agent.

2. *Identifying the elements of the offense.* Pinpointing the major components of a crime frequently reveals important leads in the investigation of a criminal case. These components include the following:
   a. Name and address of victim.
   b. Where crime was committed.
   c. Person and/or property attacked.
   d. How attacked.
   e. Means of attack.
   f. Time of attack.
   g. Object of attack.
   h. Trademark.

Together the foregoing elements of a criminal case constitute the *modus operandi* of the offender, which is discussed in greater detail later in this chapter.

3. *Detection and apprehension of the offender.* One of the major objectives of criminal investigation is to establish the identity of the offender and bring about his apprehension.

4. *The production of evidence against him.* This important phase of criminal investigation is concerned with the development of proof sufficient to sustain a conviction of the offender in a criminal court proceeding.

Most observers view criminal investigation as an art rather than a science.* They recognize the role of intuition, hunches, chance and even sheer luck in the solution of a criminal case. However, it must be conceded that it qualifies as a science to the extent that the physical and biological sciences are brought into play in the development of evidence against the criminal offender.

EQUIPMENT OF THE INVESTIGATING OFFICER

All that has been previously said concerning the selection and training of police personnel comes into sharp focus at the threshold of a criminal case investigation. Here intelligence, skill,

---

*O'Hara, Charles E.: *Fundamentals of Criminal Investigation,* Springfield, Thomas, 1956, p. 20.

enterprise, initiative, perseverance, patience, ingenuity and an insatiable curiosity, in addition to a rational method or procedure, are among the essential prerequisites to investigative success.

The Notebook

A prominent police administrator once stated that in his opinion, the most effective weapon of the officer against the criminal is his *notebook*. The ultimate objective of an investigation is to produce proof in court. It follows, therefore, that when the officer takes the witness stand, he must rely upon his memory, or some aid to memory or a combination of both. In view of the lapse of time between the investigation and the trial, he may find that his memory is uncertain and indefinite, and he may be placed in the embarrassing position of having to admit in his answers to questions that he does not know or does not remember.

The place for the notebook is in the courtroom when the case comes to trial. On the stand, it is altogether appropriate for the officer to consult his notebook to refresh his memory. As a matter of fact, the notebook is admissible in evidence. The officer's testimony is materially strengthened when it appears that at the time he ascertained the fact, he made a detailed record in his notebook. In that connection, full, complete and detailed notes should be made of every step in the investigation and of every fact or bit of information developed in the case. Furthermore, it is fundamental that all notes be recorded with a pen rather than a pencil.

Defense counsel may be permitted by the court during a trial proceeding to examine the officer's notebook. This circumstance should indicate to the investigating officer the need for using extreme care and accuracy in all notebook recording. A complete description of the crime scene is an integral part of the notebook record. It is important to observe that the notebook contains the raw material from which the investigation report is ultimately prepared.

The Investigator's Kit

In actual practice in the field, the officer will find some form of investigation kit to be very functional and useful because of the wide variety of tools and aids that may be needed during the course of a case investigation. Such kits are available on the market and are obtainable from police supply houses. However, they can be easily made by the investigating officer at relatively little expense. The dimensions of one designed and made by the author were $22'' \times 18'' \times 8''$. Consisting of two hinged sections, the portable case contained the following items:

1. Six-inch rule; one-foot rule.
2. Tape measure.
3. Six-foot rule.
4. Three-cell flashlight.
5. Extension light.
6. Adhesive tape.
7. Indelible pencil, red pencil.
8. Chalk.
9. Sealing wax.
10. Evidence labels.
11. Glass cutter.
12. Tweezers.
13. Six test tubes for receiving small particles of evidence.
14. Box of microscope specimen slides and covers.
15. Two powder atomizers.
16. Fingerprinting kit.
17. Fingerprint cards.
18. Fingerprint glass.
19. Large magnifying glass.
20. Set of keys and lock picks.
21. Drawing paper.
22. Small jimmy.
23. Envelopes.
24. Long-nosed pliers.
25. Snub-nosed pliers — wire cutters.
26. Box of thumb tacks.
27. Box of paper clips.
28. Box of paper pins.
29. Box of rubber bands.
30. Small hammer.

31. Combination screw driver.
32. Small ball of twine.
33. Small spool of wire.
34. Small cold chisel.
35. Small T-square.
36. Small triangle.
37. Fingerprint lifters.
38. Fingerprint glass.
39. Camel-hair brushes.
40. Six powder containers.
41. Ridge counter.
42. Small flat file.
43. Small regular file.
44. Inside and outside calipers.
45. Razor blade holder.
46. Small and large scissors.
47. Physician's scalpel.
48. Small spatula.

In one sense, the kit is a portable laboratory. The list of items enumerated above could, of course, be reduced or expanded. For example, a camera could be regarded as an almost indispensable addition. Every department, regardless of size, should be equipped with at least one investigation kit. As the department grows, with an increase in criminal case load and an increase in personnel strength, two or more such investigation kits would be indicated.

Where the investigative function is lodged exclusively with the patrol force, some form of investigation kit should be a part of the equipment of every patrol car. When the case load of a police department reaches a point where the assignment of one or more patrolmen in plain clothes to the detective function is indicated, the kit becomes an indispensable part of the equipment of the investigating officer.

SOURCES OF INFORMATION

It has long been recognized that sources of information are an important part of the equipment and reserve support of the investigating officer. In fact, the value of a police officer to his organization can be measured to an important degree by the nature and extent of his lines of information.

The Informer

It has been previously noted that the detective function, as it is generally understood today, first found expression in the use of informers in England and France during the sixteenth and seventeenth centuries. In a period of rapidly increasing wealth, together with weak and corrupt governmental controls, the extent of robbery, burglary and other forms of crime became a matter of major official concern. Magistrates charged with the suppression of crime recognized the need for advance information concerning the activities of criminal offenders. The circumstances suggested the advantage of buying information from informers who themselves on occasion lived outside the pale of the law.

~ The motives for revealing information to a police officer run the entire spectrum of human nature. They include vanity, civic-mindedness, fear, repentance, avoidance of punishment, gratitude or gain, revenge, jealousy and remuneration.*

On one occasion, a man who was potentially a parole violator came to the author. He revealed that he was one of three who would be involved in a safe burglary at a U. S. Post Office in a small nearby town on a certain night at 2:00 A.M. An appropriate reception committee of police personnel awaited their arrival at the appointed hour. Unfortunately, in an exchange of gunfire, the informer lost his life. As they prepared to break in the rear door of the Post Office, the leader instructed one of the three (the informer) to go across the street and "check out" a gas station where, unknown to them, two members of the receiving committee were observing developments. They could distinguish what appeared to be a forty-five automatic in his right hand as he crossed the street. Upon a command to drop the gun, he opened fire instead. The officers had no alternative but to return the compliment.

Potential informants useful to a police officer include barbers,

---

*O'Hara, Charles E., *Fundamentals of Criminal Investigation,* Springfield, Thomas, 1956, p. 135.

bartenders, beauty-shop operators, club and association secretaries, dry cleaners and laundry delivery men, employment agency personnel, garagemen, grocers, gunsmiths, hotel managers, bellboys, telephone operators, household servants, insurance investigators, janitors, window cleaners, locksmiths, milkmen, home delivery men, money-lenders, neighbors, newspaper carriers, parking lot operators, postmen, prostitutes, public utility employes, race track employes, bookmakers, rental agencies, restaurant employes, entertainers, tailors, waiters, waitresses and individuals with a known criminal record.

Informer's Privilege

In order to protect this vital source of intelligence, both the police and the informer have an understandable interest in shielding the identity of the latter. In an effort to cooperate with the police and in the interests of public safety, the United States Supreme Court has developed a rule of evidence known as the *informer's privilege* against the disclosure of his identity. But the rule and the privilege are limited, and disclosure or nondisclosure of identity pivots on the circumstances of the particular case. On the one hand, the Court is interested in protecting these lines of information; on the other, the Court is also interested in providing the accused with a fair opportunity to defend himself.*

Judicial View of Informers

In a leading case at the federal level, *Roviaro v. United States,*† the Court stated,

> What is usually referred to as the informer's privilege is, in reality, the Government's privilege to withhold from disclosure the identity of persons who furnish information of violations of law to officers charged with enforcement of that law. *Scher v. United States,* 305 U.S. 251, 254; *In re Quarles and Butler,* 158 U.S. 532; *Vogel v. Gruaz,* 110 U.S. 311, 316. The purpose of the privilege is the furtherance and protection of the public interest in effective law

---

*For a very thorough presentation in this subject area, *see* Gutterman, Melvin: *The Informer Privilege, J. Crim. L. C. & P.S., 58* (No. 1): 32.
† Roviaro v. United States, 353 U.S. 53 (1937).

enforcement. The privilege recognizes the obligation of citizens to communicate their knowledge of the commission of crimes to law-enforcement officials and, by preserving their anonymity, encourages them to perform that obligation.

. . . Most of the federal cases involving this limitation on the scope of the informer's privilege have arisen where the legality of a search without a warrant is in issue and the communications of an informer are claimed to establish probable cause. In these cases, the Government has been required to disclose the identity of the informant unless there was sufficient evidence apart from his confidential communication.

Three recent cases in the Courts of Appeals have involved the identical problem raised here — the Government's right to withhold the identity of an informer who helped to set up the commission of the crime and who was present at its occurrence. *Portomene v. United States*, 221 F.2d 582; *United States v. Conforti*, 200 F.2d 365; *Sorrentino v. United States*, 163 F.2d 627. In each case it was stated that the identity of such an informer must be disclosed whenever the informer's testimony may be relevant and helpful to the accused's defense.

We believe that no fixed rule with respect to disclosure is justifiable. The problem is one that calls for balancing the public interest in protecting the flow of information against the individual's right to prepare his defense. Whether a proper balance renders nondisclosure erroneous must depend on the particular circumstances of each case, taking into consideration the crime charged, the possible defenses, the possible significance of the informer's testimony and other relevant factors.

Most cases confirm a strong interest on the part of the courts in protecting police lines of confidential information. In *People v. Durr,** the court made the following comment:

In our consideration of this question we have been unable to perceive any necessity to hold inherent in the constitutional safeguards protecting those charged with crime the right to information completely irrelevant to the question of innocence, disclosure of which would seriously hamper effective law enforcement . . . . Considering also the deterrent aspects of the civil and criminal remedies for false arrests, it is our opinion that determination of probable cause by reliance upon the officer's testimony as to the reliability of an otherwise anonymous informer is likely to produce evils of far less consequence than those resulting from depriving the

---

*People v. Durr, 28 Ill.3d 308, 192 N.E.2d 379 (1963), *cert. denied,* 376 U.S. 973 (1964).

public of an important source of information necessary to the suppression of a particularly vicious form of crime.

Judge Gray, in *Worthington v. Scribner,** voiced the following opinion:

> It is the duty of every citizen to communicate to his government any information which he has of the commission of an offense against its laws. To encourage him in performing this duty without fear of consequences, the law holds such information to be among the secrets of state and leaves the question how far and under what circumstances the name of the informers and the channel of communication shall be suffered to be known to the absolute discretion of the government, to be exercised according to its views of what the interests of the public require. Courts of justice, therefore, will not compel or allow the discovery of such information, either by the subordinate officer to whom it is given, by the informer himself or by any other person, without the permission of the government. The evidence is excluded, not for the protection of the witness or of the party in the particular case, but upon general grounds of public policy, because of the confidential nature of such communications.

The Supreme Court of New Jersey held in *People v. Dolce,†*

> The legislative policy of New Jersey as declared by (statute) is opposed to such revelation unless the trial judge finds it is essential to a fair determination of the issue of entrapment. A frivolous demand for the information or one based only on an unsworn assertion that the defendant was seduced into perpetrating the crime by the creative activity of police officers need not be recognized . . . . The public interest to be served by preserving the free flow of information of criminal activities and by employing investigative agents who have or acquire, by deception or otherwise, access to persons engaged in such activities, should not be thwarted unless a showing is made that a defense such as entrapment is presented in good faith, with some reasonable factual support, and that the informer is a material witness necessary to the fair determination of the defense. If the rule were otherwise, a defendant by the mere naked allegation that he intended to rely on the defense could force the state to reveal the name and whereabouts of the informer and, on its refusal to do so, gain dismissal of the prosecution.

Again, in *State v. Burnett,*** the New Jersey Supreme Court reaffirmed its position in protecting police access to confidential

---

*Worthington v. Scribner, 109 Mass. 487 (1872).

†People v. Dolce 41 N.J. 422, 197 A.2d 185 (1964).

**State v. Burnett, 42 N.J. 377, 201 A.2d 39 (1964).

information:

> If a defendant may insist upon disclosure of the informant in order
> to test the truth of the officer's statement that there is an informant
> or as to what the informant related or as to the informant's reliability,
> we can be sure that every defendant will demand disclosure. He has
> nothing to lose and the prize may be the suppression of damaging
> evidence if the State cannot afford to reveal its source, as is so often
> the case. And since there is no way to test the good faith of a
> defendant who presses the demand, we must assume the routine
> demand would have to be routinely granted. The result would be that
> the State could use the informant's information only as a lead and
> could search only if it could gather adequate evidence of probable
> cause apart from the informant's data. Perhaps that approach would
> sharpen investigatorial techniques, but we doubt that there would be
> enough talent and time to cope with crime upon that basis. Rather we
> accept the premise that the informer is a vital part of society's
> defensive arsenal. The basic rule protecting his identity rests upon
> that belief.

Again, in *United States v. Fay,** the court emphasized its
interest in protecting the free flow of confidential information to
the police:

> We turn now to the crucial question of whether Coffey was
> deprived of his Fourteenth Amendment right to a fair hearing on the
> issue of probable cause because the State refused to divulge the
> informer's name. Petitioner, the State and all the courts that have
> passed on the case have treated the leading decision on the informer's
> privilege in federal prosecutions, *Roviaro v. United States,* 353 U.S.
> 53, 77 S.Ct. 623, 1 L.Ed.2d 639 (1957), as if it were fully applicable
> to state prosecutions as well. We are willing to proceed on this basis,
> as we did earlier, in our opinion, when we discussed the issue of
> probable cause, for no other view has been briefed or argued, and
> because our result is the same irrespective of whether we treat
> Roviaro as wholly relevant to state prosecutions. However, once again
> we have set forth in the margin some thoughts on the subject, in the
> hope that they may be of use in the future.
>   . . . With these principles in mind, we hold that the State was not
> required to disclose the identity of the informer in order to make use
> of the information relating to Coffey's car and his criminal record.
> This information was derived from sources wholly independent of the
> informer, even though the informer may have provided clues which

---

*United States v. Fay, 344 F.2d 625 (2d Cir. 1965).

set the independent investigation in motion. Therefore, the informer could not have given Coffey any special help in disproving or diminishing the force of Gilhofer's testimony regarding this information. See *Scher v. United States,* 305 U.S. 251, 59 S.Ct. 174, 83 L.Ed. 151 (1938); *United States v. Santiago,* 327 F.2d 573 (2 Cir. 1964).

... Typically, when the police depend upon disclosures by an informer to establish probable cause, they are also depending to a greater or lesser degree on the informer's trustworthiness. In such cases, there is particular need to scrutinize the proof of probable cause. An anonymous informer is often under strong compulsions to make false accusations, and it is all too easy for the police, without deliberately lying, to gloss these over while testifying to the informer's trustworthiness. See *Jones v. United States,* 105 U.S.App. D.C. 326, 266 F.2d 924, 928-929 (1959), (separate opinion).

... Under these circumstances, we think that petitioner's prospects of demonstrating, with the help of the informer, that he was arrested without probable cause, *are overbalanced by the State's dual interests in encouraging the free flow of confidential information* and in using probative demonstrative evidence at the trial of a suspected criminal. Therefore, we hold that the privilege exercised by the State in withholding the identity of the informer did not deprive petitioner of his Fourteenth Amendment right to a fair hearing on the issue of probable cause.

It has been held that disclosure is unnecessary unless it appears essential to show the defendant's innocence. In *United States v. Li Fat Tong:* *

It is argued that the arrest was made not only upon hearsay evidence but upon evidence derived through informers whose identity the court declined to require the government to disclose and that such an arrest was made without probable cause. Any suggestion that the evidence on which probable cause rested was derived wholly from unidentified informers, even if that fact be regarded as critical, is not borne out by the record. At the hearing of the motion to suppress, Ryan testified that he was told by the narcotic agents in Chicago that the defendant was there and was planning to leave by plane on the evening of July 8, 1944, and would arrive at LaGuardia Field at 8:30 on the morning of July 9. This proof, though based upon hearsay, was not from an informer. It is true that it was from the narcotic agent, Belmont, who received the information from an unidentified informer, that Ryan first positively learned that the defendant was

---

*United States v. Li Fat Tong, 152 F.2d 650 (2d Cir. 1945).

carrying smoking opium with him on his trip from Chicago to New York. There is no reason to suppose that hearsay evidence derived from an informer is not as competent evidence on which to show probable cause for an arrest as any other proof. The weight to be given it is a matter for the sound discretion of the court which was exercised on the motion to suppress. We hold there was no error in declining to compel the disclosure of the names of informers. For many years it has been settled law that a government official cannot be compelled to disclose the identity of an informer unless it appears upon the trial that the disclosure of the informer's name is necessary or desirable to show the prisoner's innocence. Wigmore on Evidence, 3d Ed. 2374; *Scher v. United States*, 305 U.S. 251, 253; 59 S.Ct. 174, 83 L.Ed. 151; *Marks v. Beyfus*, L.R. 25 Q.B.D. 498; *Worthington v. Scribner*, 109 Mass. 487, 12 Am.St. R.736.

The courts have repeatedly stated that disclosure or nondisclosure of the identity of an informer must be decided upon the merits and circumstances of each individual case. In this connection, the Missouri Supreme Court stated in *State v. Bailey:**

> It would simplify matters if the question of divulgence or nondivulgence of the identity of an informant could be finally ruled one way or the other so as to apply to all cases.
>
> ...It is clear, however, that if due regard be given to the demands of justice to the public on the one hand and the constitutional rights of the defendant on the other, each case must be considered on its own merits ....
>
> The question of whether the disclosure of the identity of a nonparticipating informant is essential to assure a fair determination of the issue in any given criminal case, is for the trial court in the first instance.

That of the informer is a dangerous business. On occasion, they make the front pages in a violent death at the hands of gunmen. In addition to himself, the informer must, of course, think of his family.

The Court held in *Rugendorf v. United States†* that disclosure was not required because the defense failed to raise the question in the lower court. A similar opinion was given in the Conforti case:

> Petitioner also contends that the withholding of the identities of the informants was a sufficient ground to require suppression of the evidence. But in *Jones, supra,* we said that "as hearsay alone does not

---

*State v. Bailey, 320 Mo. 271, 8 S.W.2d 57 (1928).
† Rugendorf v. United States, 376 U.S. 528 (1964).

render an affidavit insufficient, the Commissioner need not have required the informants . . . to be produced . . . so long as there was a substantial basis for crediting the hearsay."

. . . Petitioner also asserts that he was entitled to the name of the informer who reported seeing the furs in his basement in order to defend himself at trial on the merits. This claim was not properly raised in the trial court nor passed upon there, and, accordingly, must be denied here.

. . . The necessity for disclosure depends upon "the particular circumstances of each case, taking into consideration the crime charged, the possible defenses, the possible significance of the informer's testimony, and other relevant factors." 353 U.S. 53, 62. Petitioner did not develop any such criteria with reference to the merits of the case. On the contrary, a careful examination of the whole record shows that he requested the informers' names only in his attack on affidavit supporting the search warrant. Having failed to develop the criteria of *Roviaro* necessitating disclosure on the merits, we cannot say on this record that the name of the informant was necessary to his defense. All petitioner's demands for identification of the informants were made during the hearings on the motion to suppress and were related to that motion. Never did petitioner's counsel indicate how the informants' testimony could help establish petitioner's innocence.

In *Eberhart v. United States,* * failure of the government to produce an informer, once he is identified, does not violate the defendant's rights.

Petitioner's final contention is that the Government was required to produce Ambrose as a witness and the failure to do so violated the constitutional right of the accused to be faced by his accuser. Ambrose, according to petitioner, visited Eberhart's apartment and gave petitioner $360 in marked currency. But the failure of the Government to produce an informer or person as witness does not violate defendant's rights. *Curtis v. Rivera,* U.S. App. D.C. 66, 123 F.2d 936; Check *Quong v. United States* 82 App. D.C. 8, 160 F.2d 251. The Government has no duty to place on the witness stand every person with some knowledge of the circumstances.

The courts have ruled that where disclosure is indicated, the defense is entitled to know not only his name but to receive information concerning his whereabouts and reasonable cooperation in making him available to the defense. For example,

---

*Eberhart v. United States, 262 F.2d 421 (9th Cir. 1958).

in *United States v. D'Angiolillo,* *

The defendants first argue that the court should have directed the government to call Greene as a witness or itself have called him. We have considered this problem in a number of cases, e.g. *United States v. White,* 2 Cir., 324 F.2d 814, 816 (1963); *United States v. Cimino,* 321 F.2d 509, 512 (1963), cert. denied, *D'Ercole v. United States,* 375 U.S. 967, 974, 84 S.Ct. 486, 11 L.Ed.2d 416 (1964); *United States v. Holiday,* 2 Cir., 319 F.2d 775 (1963). The rule emerging from these and earlier decisions is that where the informer's testimony may be relevant to the defense, the defendant is entitled to his name, to such information as the government may have concerning his whereabouts† and to reasonable cooperation in securing his appearance.

. . . Greene was readily available, being confined in the New York City Penitentiary Prison, and Judge Cannella offered to have him served with a subpoena. He also offered to permit defendants to interrogate Greene privately before deciding whether to call him as a witness and told them that they could question him as a hostile witness if such he proved to be. The defendants chose not to call him but instead advised the court to do so after the government rested its case without calling Greene. There is no basis whatever for their claim that there was error in the government's failure and the court's refusal to call Greene.

The defendants cite no case holding that the court is required to direct the government to call the informer or to call him as a witness of the court, and, at least on the facts of this case, we see no reason for imposing such a duty.

In a number of cases, it has been held that where a reliable informant supplies information which to some extent has been corroborated in the course of the officer's investigation, disclosure is not required.**

The credibility of an informant and the method or methods for determining credibility have occupied the attention of the courts in a number of cases. For example, the informant's criminal record, current criminal activities, addiction to narcotics and

---

*United States v. D'Angiolillo, 340 F.2d 453 (2d Cir. 1965), *cert. denied,* 380 U.S. 955 (1965).

†See our opinion in *United States v. Comulada,* 2 Cir., 340 F.2d 449, filed today. Of course, where the informer or his family might be endangered by public disclosure, the trial court in its discretion may direct that the information be revealed only to counsel, as done in this case.

**United States, *ex. rel.* Coffey v. Fay, 344 F.2d 103, F.2d 625 (2d Cir. 1965).

motive for passing on the information to an officer may operate as factors supporting credibility.*

Probable cause for an arrest may be satisfied in part by information from a reliable informant, and it is unnecessary to disclose his identity. This has been indicated in a number of cases, including *People v. Durr.*†

In general, rules set forth by state courts concerning the informer privilege follow a similar pattern to those developed at the federal level, as indicated in the following cases.

The Alabama Supreme Court ruled that

> a government official cannot be compelled to disclose the name of an informer. But there is an exception recognized by the cases based on constitutional grounds, which is that if it appears that the informer's name is necessary or desirable to show the prisoner's innocence, the official can be required by the court to make disclosure.**

The same court held in *Roach v. State,*

> We do not believe an employee of the Federal Government carries about him a mantle such as the Roman citizenship that shielded the Apostle Paul from the municipal law. Hence, we do not conceive that the superintendency in *Rea v. U.S.* operates to such an extent as to make the principle (of requiring the disclosure of the name of a participating decoy) in *Roviaro v. U.S.,* become the law of Alabama when a Federal witness testifies in a state court regarding a state crime.††

In California, disclosure of the identity of an informer is not limited to one who participates in the alleged crime. The California Supreme Court stated in *People v. McShann,*¶

> The information elicited from an informer may be "relevant and helpful to the defense of the accused or essential to a fair determination of a cause," even though the informer was not a participant.
> . . . When it appears from the evidence, however, that the informer is also a material witness on the issue of guilt, his identity is relevant and may be helpful to the defendant. Nondisclosure would deprive

---

*McCoy v. State, 216 Md. 332, 140 A.2d 689 (1958), *cert. denied,* 358 U.S. 853 (1958).
†People v. Durr, 28 Ill.2d 308, 192 N.E.2d 379 (1963), *cert. denied,* 376 U.S. 973 (1964).
**Parson v. State, 251 Ala. 467, 38 So.2d 209 (1948).
††Roach v. State, 39 Ala. App. 271, 97 So.2d 837 (1957).
¶ People v. McShann, 50 Cal.2d 802, 330 P.2d 33 (1958).

him of a fair trial.

... The informer's telephone call was persuasive evidence on possession, for it indicated that the defendant was en route to make a sale of heroin when he was arrested and therefore knowingly had possession at that time. As the originator of the telephone call, the informer was a material witness on the issue of possession. The prosecution made him such a witness by introducing evidence of his telephone call to make a purchase of heroin and by playing a recording of the telephone conversation before the jury.

The same court held in *Priestly v. Superior Court,* *

If testimony of communications from a confidential informer is necessary to establish the legality of a search, the defendant must be given a fair opportunity to rebut that testimony. He must therefore be permitted to ascertain the identity of the informer, since legality of the officer's action depends upon the credibility of the information, not upon facts that he directly witnessed and upon which he could be cross-examined.

The court further stated,

If a search is made pursuant to a warrant valid on its face and the only objection is that it was based on information given to a police officer by an unnamed informant, there is substantial protection against unlawful search and the necessity of applying the exclusionary rule in order to remove the incentive to engage in unlawful searches is not present. The warrant, of course, is issued by a magistrate, not by a police officer, and will be issued only when the magistrate is satisfied by the supporting affidavit that there is probable cause. He may, if he sees fit, require disclosure of the identity of the informer before issuing the warrant or require that the informant be brought to him. The requirement that an affidavit be presented to the magistrate and his control over the issuance of the warrant diminish the danger of illegal action, and it does not appear that there has been frequent abuse of the search-warrant procedure. One of the purposes of the adoption of the exclusionary rule was to further the use of warrants, and it obviously is not desirable to place unnecessary burdens upon their use. The additional protection which would result from application of the Priestly rule in situations such as the one involved here would not offset the disadvantages of excluding probative evidence of crime and obstructing the flow of information to police.

The situation in Illinois is reflected in *People v. Durr,*† the leading case on the informer privilege in that state. The Illinois

---

*Priestly v. Superior Court, 50 Cal. 2d at 809, 330 P.2d at 37.
†People v. Durr, see p. 34.

Supreme Court reaffirmed *Durr* in *People v. McCary,** holding,

> (W)e believe that an accused is afforded constitutional protection against unreasonable search and seizure if the State is compelled to support a search incidental to an arrest without a search warrant by credible evidence showing the basis for reasonable cause by the arresting officer. We do not believe that it is necessary to bare the identity of every informant assisting society in its struggle against the narcotic traffic in order to preserve the fundamental guarantees of the Constitution. Otherwise the so-called informant's privilege and its value would disappear.

In Maine, the Supreme Judicial Court commented in *State v. Fortin,†*

> It is a well-settled rule that a defendant upon the trial of an indictment against him is not entitled as of right to know who gave the information or made the complaints which started the prosecution. Such communications to officers of the law should ordinarily be regarded as privileged as to the identity of the informant or complainant on the ground of public policy, so that no one from fear of consequences to him personally shall hesitate to give information of offenses.

The Supreme Court in Ohio expressed the view in *State v. Beck*** that

> Only in an instance where an informer's identity would be beneficial and helpful to a defendant is there any basis for requiring disclosure . . . . The revelation of the name of the informer and the information supplied by him would not alter the fact of defendant's guilt. And a mere desire to test the credibility and reliability of the informer is hardly a compelling consideration in the circumstances narrated.

Texas takes a firm stand on the informer privilege in favor of the police. In *Bridges v. State,††* the Court of Criminal Appeals observed,

> an Officer is not required to reveal the name of the person from whom he receives information upon which he bases his right to arrest or search upon probable cause.

In a later case, *Artell v. Texas,¶* the court ruled,

---

*People v. McCray, 33 Ill.2d 66, 210 N.E.2d 161 (1965).
†State v. Fortin, 106 Me. 382, 76 A.896 (1910).
**State v. Beck, 175 Ohio St. 73, 191 N.E.2d 825 (1963).
††Bridges v. State, 166 Tex. Crime 556, 316 S.W.2d 757 (1958).
¶ Artell v. Texas,

the court did not err in declining to require . . . (the officer) to name his informer. This is especially so since there is no showing that the informant took any material part in bringing about the offense, was present when it occurred or might be a material witness as to whether or not accused committed the offense.

The Supreme Court of Tennessee made the following comment in *Smith v. State:**

> (W)hen an officer seeks to justify an arrest upon a charge made upon reasonable cause, the officer should be required to reveal the identity of the person making the charge as well as the nature of the charge. The Court has to pass upon the officer's justification, and that justification is open to impeachment. A defendant should not be bound by the officer's statement that a charge had been made, and, unless the source of the charge is ascertained, neither its good faith nor reality could well be challenged. An unscrupulous officer, upon a fictitious story of a "charge made," might vindicate any arrest, however unlawful, if there could be no further inquiry.

An attempt was made in *Lewis v. United States†* to exploit the Escobedo doctrine in claiming an unlawful search and seizure because a government agent posing as a customer misled the defendant as to his true identity. The First Circuit Court of Appeals handed down the following opinion:

> Defendant, convicted of selling marijuana to a government agent who had misrepresented his identity, claims an unlawful search and seizure because, thus misled by the agent, he invited him to his home and there made the sale. The happy days for law violators that this claim would produce are not to be . . . His reliance upon *Escobedo v. State of Illinois* . . . is quite misplaced.

However, this case is now on appeal to the Supreme Court.**

In the foregoing decisions, it can be seen that the basic interest of the courts in protecting this vital flow of confidential information has tilted the scales somewhat in favor of the police and the informer.

Other Sources

There are unlimited sources of information available to a police

---

*Smith v. State 169 Tenn. 633, 90 S.W.2d 523 (1936).
†Lewis v. United States, 352 F.2d 799 (1st Cir. 1965).

officer other than the services of an informer. For a complete, classified inventory of these sources, the reader is referred to the excellent work, *Criminal Investigation*, by Charles E. O'Hara, published by Charles C Thomas, Publisher, Springfield, Illinois. This book should be in the library of every police department. Routine sources of information at the disposal of every police officer include federal records, state, county and municipal records, private agencies' records and other miscellaneous sources.

Federal Records

War Department — Office of the Adjutant General. The Office of the Adjutant General maintains records of all organizations, officers and enlisted personnel that are, or have been, in the military service of the United States.

Service commands. The Security and Intelligence Divisions of the various service command headquarters maintain records which may be of assistance to the investigator.

Provost marshals. Provost marshals at posts, camps, or stations, and at overseas establishments, also maintain records concerning military personnel.

Navy Department — The Office of Naval Intelligence.

Department of Justice — The Federal Bureau of Investigation. The incomparable resources of the Federal Bureau of Investigation, including the criminal and civilian fingerprint files, are well known to every police officer in the country.

The Immigration and Naturalization Service. This organization maintains files which include the photographs, fingerprints, and brief biographies of aliens and immigrants, their residence and employment addresses, and the status of their naturalization. To aid in identifying the subject, the investigator should provide the Immigration and Naturalization Service with the name of the vessel, the date and the port of entry if this information can be obtained.

Treasury Department Investigative Agencies. These agencies have important information on file; they include the following:

The United States Secret Service.

The Bureau of Narcotics.

The Intelligence Unit Bureau of the Internal Revenue Service.

The Alcohol Tax Unit Bureau of the Internal Revenue Service.

The Bureau of Customs.

The Post Office Department. This department will usually provide the investigating officer with all the information which appears on the outside of envelopes in the United States mail addressed to a particular individual. This service is known as a "mail cover" and will be continued for a specific period agreed upon by the investigator and the postal authorities.

Division of Investigations, Department of the Interior.

Wages and Hours Division, Labor Department.

The Veterans Administration. They have on file information relating to former members of the military naval forces.

The United States Maritime Commission. This group maintains records concerning the activities of the Merchant Marine and its officers and crews.

The Department of State. The department has complete information relating to passports and visas.

The Federal Communications Commission. The F.C.C. investigates and reports on all organizations engaged in interstate radio or wire communications, and licenses and monitors all radio stations.

State, County and Municipal Records

Among the various records which may have information of value to the investigating officers are those of the following:

State police and highway patrols.

Local police departments.

Office of the State Attorney General.

Sheriff's office.

Fish and Game Wardens.

Coroners or medical examiners.

Fire marshals.

City attorney or city prosecutor.

County district attorney or prosecutor.
Health, sanitation, building and license inspectors.
Truant officers.
Public welfare and social service agencies.
Penal and probationary agencies.
Courts.
Tax assessors and collectors.
Public and private schools, colleges and universities.
County clerks, city clerks.
Marriage license bureaus.

Private Agencies' Records

The American Red Cross.
Commercial credit bureaus. They maintain extensive files on persons who have made use of personal credit. These files include addresses, bank accounts, charge accounts, records of judgment, assets and financial standing.
Insurance company clearing house. The National Association of Life Underwriters, 11 West 42nd Street, New York City, and various civilian credit agencies have records on all persons who have or have had an interest in life insurance policies. The National Board of Fire Underwriters, 85 John Street, New York City, has the same information with regard to fire insurance policies.
Railroad companies. Railroad companies and their railroad police are cooperative in furnishing information relative to the place of departure and destination of individuals and shipments.
Bus lines. Bus companies maintain bills of lading at points of shipment and transfer points.
Steamship companies and airlines. These companies usually have records of the names and addresses of passengers, the dates of travel, the point of disembarkation for each passenger and the reservations made for land transportation and hotel accommodations.
Telephone companies. Telephone companies maintain records of long-distance calls, showing the number calling and the city

and number called. On certain calls, the name of the caller and the name and address of the person called are recorded.

Telegraph companies. Telegraph companies have records and copies of telegrams and money orders.

Water, electric and gas companies. These groups are often the first agencies to obtain the addresses and names of persons who recently arrived in a city.

Newspaper files. Newspapers maintain what are commonly called "morgues," which disclose the extent and type of publicity which an individual has received.

Real estate agencies. These people have information concerning their tenants and real estate transactions.

Automobile associations. Automobile associations can furnish information concerning the registration and ownership of the automobiles of their members.

State Motor Vehicle Departments. These departments have complete information concerning all automobiles they have licensed.

Hospitals. All hospitals keep records of wounds, injuries, illnesses, scars, births and deaths.

Local Bureaus of Vital Statistics. These groups also maintain records covering births and deaths.

Hotel associations. Hotel associations maintain files on criminals such as worthless check operators, card sharks, bunco operators and confidence men. By inquiring at the association's office, the investigating officer may obtain information concerning any guest of a member hotel.

Miscellaneous Records

Telephone directories. These are arranged alphabetically according to the names of the subscribers, or according to the business of the subscriber in the classified section. Special telephone directories are compiled for large businesses and other agencies, arranged according to street address.

City directories. A city directory will furnish addresses, occupations, names and members of families living in the city at the time information for the directory was collected. Early editions will reveal the year a person moved into the locality, former addresses and occupations.

The foregoing, somewhat abridged, list of sources of information available to the investigating officer suggests the wide diversity and extent of coverage a case investigation may take in the search for evidence.

IV

THE CARE AND PRESERVATION
OF EVIDENCE

NATURE OF EVIDENCE

EVIDENCE is that which sustains proof or denies it. It includes testimony on the witness stand, records, documents, objects, scientifically established facts and other data that can be legally presented during a criminal trial for the purpose of assisting the court and jury in arriving at a determination concerning the truth of the issue involved.

Evidence falls into two major classifications — direct and circumstantial. Direct evidence is the testimony of an eyewitness and is the weakest and most unreliable of all types of evidence. It can be perjured and is subject to all of the frailties of human memory and the senses of perception.

Circumstantial evidence, the most reliable of all, is concerned with a scientifically validated fact which speaks for itself, such as the identification of a bloody fingerprint on a butcher knife or a laboratory determination that a fatal bullet recovered from the body of the victim was fired from a revolver which was in possession of the suspect at the time of his arrest. The total yield from a crime detection laboratory qualifies as circumstantial evidence.

Some observers draw a distinction between circumstantial evidence and what is referred to as real or physical evidence. Within this frame of reference, circumstantial evidence establishes a certain fact or series of facts which tend to prove certain elements of the case and would not include the bloody butcher knife or the identified revolver. They would be catalogued as real or physical evidence.

The distinction is confusing and falls somewhat short of the test for validity. Webster defines circumstance as a condition, fact or event accompanying, conditioning or determining another condition, fact or event. An identified bloody fingerprint or a gun identified as having fired the fatal bullet is a *circumstance* which tends to, or does, sustain proof of the fact. It is convenient and useful, therefore, in looking at the investigative process, to consider evidence as either direct or circumstantial.

THE CRIME SCENE SEARCH

In certain categories of crime, including all crimes of violence — homicides, assaults, robbery, burglary and certain other forms of theft — the search of the crime scene can easily prove to be the most important part of the investigation. Wherever there has been an impact of the offender upon the crime environment, the crime scene search becomes a matter of overwhelming importance.

It would be extremely difficult for an individual to merely walk into and out of a room without leaving some evidence behind that he had been there and without taking some evidence with him that he had been there. The criminal impact is such that the chances for this displacement of matter, whether large or microscopic, is multiplied many times. The evidence resources of the crime scene are such that a thorough search is mandatory.

Protection of the Crime Scene

One of the major responsibilities of the first officer arriving at the scene is to prevent the destruction or contamination of evidence and to initiate security measures to prevent unauthorized persons from entering the area. The crime scene search should then be conducted on a systematic basis using the grid, quadrant or other method to assure that no part of the area is overlooked or neglected.

If the investigating officer has not received complete training in the development of latent fingerprints, making casts and molds, photographing crime scenes, handling evidence and other scientific crime-detection techniques, he should merely protect the area until another officer with the prerequisite training and experience arrives. It goes without saying that the training of every police officer should include techniques of the crime-scene search and the care and preservation of evidence.

Upon arrival at the scene of a criminal offense, the investigating officer should stop and observe the area as a whole, noting everything he can see before he enters the area to make a detailed examination. A photograph from this point is of the greatest value as a record to show the court exactly how the crime scene first appeared to the investigator.

Recording the Crime Scene

Before examining the area in detail, the officer should record the time of arrival at the scene and note the weather conditions. In addition, he should do the following:

1. Prohibit all persons who witnessed or who are acquainted with the circumstances of the crime from leaving the area until their names and addresses have been obtained; all of them should be questioned in detail.
2. Remove all persons from the room or immediate vicinity to prevent the destruction of evidence.
3. Isolate the scene of the crime by locking entrances and where necessary, by posting guards or roping off the area to prevent the entrance of unauthorized persons.

The area should be permanently recorded by describing the scene and evidence in the officer's notebook and photographing the scene, in addition to making sketches.

It is imperative that the investigating officer record in his notebook the results of his search of the crime scene and the results of his examination of witnesses. The details of his examination of objects, as well as suggestions, leads and other information obtained by interviews should be entered in detail in his notebook. As previously indicated, the information recorded in his notebook may be used by the investigating officer while on the witness stand to refresh his memory.

Photographs present a valuable and permanent record of the crime scene. Many cases have been unsuccessfully prosecuted because an accurate photograph of the scene was not taken. For each photograph made, the investigating officer should record in his notebook the exact location and angle of the camera with respect to the scene; the name, make and model of the camera, lighting conditions, type of film, lens opening, diaphragm setting and shutter speed for each photographic exposure.

After completing photographic coverage, the investigating officer should:

1. Prepare a sketch of the crime scene showing the location, approaches and entrances of the building or area; the size and number of rooms; the location of fingerprints, footprints or tracks; what objects were on the floor, ceiling or walls; whether windows or doors were open or closed; and all other physical descriptions pertinent to the case.

2. The angle and location of the camera should be indicated in the sketch so that the photographs and sketch may be tied together.

3. The sketch and the description of objects in the officer's notebook should include the date and hour when they were made and the signature of the investigating officer.

4. The sketch must always indicate the compass direction and scale. All measurements should be made with care and accuracy. No changes should be made on the original sketch after the officer has left the scene.

5. The sketch should be drawn first to show content and then be redrawn to scale. Recommended scales are: 1/2 inch on the sketch equal to 1 foot in ordinary rooms; 1/8 inch on the sketch equal to 10 feet in larger areas. Within these limits, a satisfactory scale may be selected. The original rough sketch made at the scene should be preserved even after it has been redrawn so that it will be available if needed in court.

6. Objects shown in the sketch should be designated by numbers, letters or symbols, described accurately and referred to by their designations in the officer's notebook.

If the offense was committed in a room, the officer should first observe the floor at the principal point of entrance to the room, then minutely examine the entire floor for possible stains, traces, marks, scratches or objects. The larger objects should also be carefully examined even though they may appear to be unrelated to the case under investigation. The investigating officer may then, starting at one corner of the room, carefully examine the walls, doors and windows for the purpose of determining the probable direction of the offender's entry and exit. The contents of all articles of furniture and containers, such as wastebaskets and drawers, should be carefully noted, with letters and memoranda read and listed in the officer's notebook. Care should be exercised in handling any papers or objects which may bear latent fingerprints.

The terrain about the premises should be methodically examined for traces of the movements of the offender such as damaged vegetation, disturbance of the soil, footprints and objects which may have been dropped by the offender. Where a body is found at the scene, its position, including such parts as the head, hands, feet and trunk, and its relation to other surrounding objects, should be sketched and described in the officer's notebook. It is suggested that the examination of the body begin at the head, observing the head covering, if any, and the color, length, arrangement and contents of the hair.

Observe the face for injuries, blood, dirt, extraneous matter, distinctive marks, the position of the eyes and mouth, and the expression. Note whether the hands are clean or dirty, open or clenched, as well as the position of the fingers or the presence of a ring. It may be desirable to remove matter under the fingernails for analysis. The clothing of the body should be noted for its arrangement or disarrangement, degree of cleanliness, whether it is wet or dry, its material, quality, color, pattern and name of maker. Clothing should later be removed from the body for laboratory examination. Matter may be removed from the cracks of the shoes and from the space between the upper and the sole. The examination should include the back of the body and the ground or floor under it. Whenever possible, it is advisable to examine the body with the assistance of a licensed physician. Before the body is removed, its position should be outlined on the floor in chalk.

All appropriate surfaces should be examined for latent finger-prints and when they are portable, they should be transported with appropriate care to headquarters. Where this is impractical, any latent fingerprints developed should be photographed and the print protected for further reference.

In terms of portability and transportation to police headquarters, the author was involved in the investigation of an attempted safe burglary in the offices of a produce company. An examination of the safe door revealed a number of holes had been drilled in the immediate vicinity of the combination dial. The beam of a flashlight plainly showed that a drill had been broken and was still imbedded in one of the holes. Permission was obtained from the owner of the company to take the safe door to headquarters where it was demolished and the piece of drill recovered. The companion piece of the drill was found the same day in a bag of burglary tools in the possession of a suspect who had been taken into custody. The two pieces of drill were never used in evidence because of the untimely death of the suspect. He was a drug addict and was taken to the county hospital for treatment later in the evening. During the night, he broke into the nurses' quarters and inadvertently took an overdose of morphine.

Evidence in most cases should not be moved until it has been photographed and processed for latent fingerprints, listed and described in the officer's notebook and plotted on the sketch. When moved, the evidence should be properly tagged and marked for identification. In connection with objects bearing latent fingerprints, elimination prints should be taken of all persons who had normal access to the object or article.

PRESERVING EVIDENCE

There are important rules to be followed in the care and preservation of evidence. The following instructions were prepared by the author for a field manual covering the preparation of evidence materials for shipment to a crime laboratory for examination and analysis. They apply with equal force to the moving of evidence from the scene to police headquarters.

1. In the handling of physical evidence, it is important that it reach the laboratory in as nearly as possible the same condition as that in which it was found at the scene of the crime, on the person of the suspect, etc.
2. The courts have held repeatedly that evidence must be identified with the place of discovery and must show a

complete chain of custody. The investigator must be in a position to prove the continuous possession of evidence from the time of the discovery until its introduction as evidence in the trial of the case. It is desirable that evidence pass through the custody of as few persons as possible. *Send evidence to the laboratory as soon after discovery as possible.*

3. Evidence material should be packed for shipment so as not to move about in the container while in transit.
4. Each article should be wrapped separately **and labeled.** If a number of articles are to be forwarded to the laboratory, each must be wrapped separately and labeled, but all may be placed in a larger container for shipment, and sealed.
5. Evidence submitted for latent fingerprint examination should be packed so that nothing comes into contact with the surfaces upon which the suspected latent fingerprints may appear.
6. Liquids should be placed in well-stoppered vials or containers, properly labeled, and then packed so as to avoid breakage or leakage in transit.
7. Wet stains upon cloth, paper or other objects should be air dried before packing to avoid putrefaction in transit. Do not put in draft, under fan or use artificial heat to dry it.
8. Powder, dust, hairs, specks of paint and other small particles of evidence require special care. Such small specimens may be collected in a clean pill box, sealed with tape and properly labeled. Or, they may be collected on a clean sheet of white paper; the paper is then folded in a manner known as the druggists' fold for powder prescriptions, sealed and placed in an envelope, which is then sealed and properly labeled. Never place evidence loose in an envelope.
9. Be sure that all containers are sealed.
10. Be sure that each item of evidence is properly marked and labeled so that it may be identified by the investigator when introduced in court.

Latent Fingerprint Evidence

1. Articles such as weapons of attack, tools, documents, glass, metal and objects which could have been touched or handled by the suspect in a criminal case may be forwarded to the laboratory for latent fingerprint examination. Articles submitted to the laboratory for this purpose will be dusted, fumed or chemically treated for the development of latent fingerprints, depending upon the nature of the material submitted.

2. Considerable care is necessary in preparing latent fingerprint evidence for shipment in order to avoid adding fingerprints to the evidence or destroying those already present. This type of evidence should be packed so that nothing touches the suspected area. Do not wrap such articles in cloth or paper, or wedge paper against them in a box.

3. Weapons of attack, including firearms, may be successfully prepared for shipment by placing the object on its side on the bottom of a strong corrugated cardboard box. Lace the object in place by punching holes around it and sewing it down with heavy twine to immobilize the specimen, being careful to avoid any contact with the suspected areas as far as possible. Pack object thus prepared in a larger container, seal, label and send it to the laboratory.

4. Bottles and other similar objects to be examined for latent fingerprints may be prepared for shipment in the following manner: outline base end of bottle with a pencil on a piece of wood; pound nails around this line so as to provide a support for the bottle. Follow same procedure for neck-end of bottle. Place ends in position and fasten together by means of wood strips running from end to end. Pack in a suitable container of proper size, seal, label and forward to laboratory.

5. Flat articles such as mirrors, glass plate (particularly window pane glass) and metal plate may be prepared for shipment by sandwiching article between two pieces of

plywood or heavy, stiff cardboard, providing for at least one inch clearance above suspected area or areas. Label and pack securely in larger container, seal and transmit to laboratory.

6. If the object bearing latent prints cannot be removed or sent to the laboratory, arrange to have the print or prints photographed locally. Be sure to include a scale or portion of a ruler in photograph. The suspected area should then be protected for future reference. *Do not attempt to "lift" a fingerprint if this can be avoided.*

7. As with other types of evidence, the laboratory is in a position to prepare suitable photographic exhibits for investigative and court purposes.

Processing Fingerprints of Unknown Deceased Persons

Law enforcement officers are frequently called upon to fingerprint unknown deceased persons in an effort to establish identification. In most cases, little difficulty is experienced in obtaining a suitable set of prints for identification purposes.

In a number of instances, however, such as drowning, fire, or long exposure to the elements, etc., decomposition or destruction of tissue may have occurred, making it extremely difficult to obtain identifiable fingerprint impressions. The laboratory is equipped to assist law enforcement officials in such cases. In situations of this kind, it is suggested that the local health officer or a licensed physician be properly authorized to remove the hands from the human body by severing them at the wrist. *Do not sever fingers.*

The hands may be placed in a glass jar of suitable size containing a 5% solution of formaldehyde, sealed, labeled and packed carefully in a suitable container to avoid breakage and sent to the laboratory. If any difficulty is experienced regarding the proper procedure in a particular case, it is suggested that the laboratory be contacted by telephone. Through proper processing of the fingers in such cases, it is frequently possible to obtain fingerprints suitable for identification purposes, even though decomposition has set in.

Clothing

1. Clothing of the victim or suspect offers one of the most productive sources of information and clues for the investigator in a criminal case. Microscopic and chemical examinations of clothing often reveal important information.

2. Do not shake or in any way attempt to clean articles of clothing being sent to the laboratory for examination. Often dust in clothing, in the cuffs of trousers, from the pockets and from gloves is of the greatest assistance.

3. Do not cut away a section of clothing for transmittal to the laboratory; send the complete garment or garments.

4. Attach to each piece of clothing a tag containing all identifying data. If more than one garment, each piece of clothing must be wrapped separately to avoid contamination of one piece by the other, but all may be placed in a suitable larger container, sealed and labeled for shipment to the laboratory.

5. If clothing is wet or damp, place it on clothes hangers and allow it to air dry before packing. Do not put in a draft, under a fan or use artificial heat to dry it.

6. If gunshot or powder patterns are suspected, a piece of clean white paper should be placed on either side of the suspected area. Folds of the cloth in wrapping should not be made through this area.

7. For handling blood and seminal stains found on clothing, refer to specific instructions on those subjects in another section.

Weapons and Instruments of Attack

1. Under laboratory examination, weapons of attack of all types in assaults and homicides, and instruments of attack against property, as in burglary, may yield significant information.

2. Weapons and instruments of attack submitted to the laboratory will be examined to determine the presence of

hairs, fibers, stains, latent fingerprints, imbedded foreign material and other characteristics which may link the object with the crime and with the suspect.

Document Examination

1. The investigation of criminal cases frequently pivots upon the examination and identification of handwriting, handprinting, typewriting, papers, inks, seals, water marks, erasures, obliterated writing and alterations in documents.
2. Considerable care must be exercised in preparing checks, notes, letters and other suspected documents for transmittal to the laboratory.
3. Whether the suspected document be a worthless check, a forged suicide note or an anonymous letter, *handle it as little as possible. It may bear valuable fingerprint evidence.*
4. The original suspected document must be forwarded to the laboratory. Photographic or photostat copies of the original document are *not* acceptable. The laboratory is equipped to make the necessary photographic reproductions for examination and for use in court.
5. It is best not to place a mark of identification on the original document. This may be done on another piece of paper and clipped to the original document. Place in a cellophane envelope to prevent handling. Sandwich this envelope between two sheets of stiff cardboard; tape cardboards together with adhesive strips; label, wrap or place in manila envelope and forward to the laboratory. However, two or more cellophane envelopes may be forwarded together in the above manner. Do not add any folds or creases to the original document.
6. Document examinations require comparison with known genuine standards. Genuine standards in sufficient quantity should be forwarded to the laboratory with the original suspected document or documents. The following brief suggestions will prove useful to the investigator:

a. In cases involving handwriting or handprinting, it is usually possible for the investigator to observe whether the writing was made with indelible pencil, black lead pencil (hard or soft), fountain pen, or pen and staff. It is important to note also whether the writing was on ruled or unruled paper.

   Standards for comparison written by the suspect should be made with the same kind of writing instrument and on the same general type of paper as that used on the questioned document. In check cases, blank checks are useful for this purpose. Have the suspect write several specimens. Remove each sample from his sight before making the next.

b. It is frequently possible to obtain known genuine standards of the suspect's writing from other sources, such as letters, cancelled checks, legal documents, diaries, etc., where they are of approximately the same date as the suspected writing. However, writing by the suspect under observation of the officer is best. As a general rule, little or no difficulty is experienced in obtaining the cooperation of the suspect.

c. If the suspected document is typewritten, sample typewriting specimens should be obtained from the suspected typewriter or typewriters, if known. However, laboratory examination of a typewritten document may reveal important information even though the suspected typewriter is unknown.

d. All standard writing specimens should be properly marked for identification, placed in envelopes and sealed. They may be forwarded in the same container with the original suspected document.

e. Papers possess numerous identifying characteristics which may prove useful to the investigator. Ink used in the writing of a suspected document may be examined for composition, type, erasures and alterations.

f. Examination of mechanical writing made by check protectors, rubber stamps and printing may also prove important in certain cases.

Firearms Identification

The laboratory maintains complete facilities for the examination of firearms evidence in criminal cases. Under laboratory examination, it may be possible to provide the investigator with an answer to one or more of the following questions:

From what type or make of firearm was the fatal bullet fired?

Was the fatal bullet fired from the suspected gun?

In what type or make of firearm was a discharged cartridge case fired?

Was the discharged cartridge case fired in the suspected gun?

Were two or more bullets fired from the same firearm?

Were two or more cartridge cases fired in the same firearm?

What type of powder was used in the ammunition?

At approximately what distance from the victim was the fatal shot fired? and from what direction?

The following precautions should be observed by the investigator in forwarding firearms evidence to the laboratory:

1. Unload the suspected gun before packing for shipment. Never submit a loaded gun to the laboratory. From automatics, remove clip from gun and remove cartridge from the chamber. In the case of revolvers, remove all cartridges from the cylinder. Make a note of the exact position of each cartridge, both fired and unfired, in the cylinder, and send this information to the laboratory with the evidence.

2. Never attempt to clean the bore, chamber or cylinder, and do not wipe off the outside of the suspected gun.

3. Use every precaution to avoid destruction of fingerprint evidence which may be present on the weapon. With careful handling of the gun, the officer will be able to unload it without mutilating fingerprint evidence.

4. Record the serial number and make of the firearm. Place upon it your mark of identification.

5. Prepare for shipment by placing gun on its side on the bottom of a strong corrugated cardboard or pasteboard box; lace gun in place by punching holes around it and sewing it down with strong twine.

6. Pack in a larger carton so as to avoid contact with surfaces on gun which might bear fingerprint evidence; seal, label and forward to the laboratory.

7. Do not fire test shots. All test shots from suspected gun should be fired in the laboratory.

8. Cartridges, bullets, cases and clips should be marked for identification as follows:
   a. *Fired Bullets.* Mark only on base end (never on side or nose) with your initial.
   b. *Cartridge Cases.* Mark only on inside of open end, never on closed end.
   c. *Unfired Cartridges.* Mark on side of case near bullet end.
   d. *Clips.* Mark on side of clip.

9. Cartridges, bullets and cases should be prepared for transmittal to the laboratory as follows: Pack each cartridge, bullet or fired cartridge case in a separate pill box with cotton, pack tightly enough to immobilize the specimen, seal, label and forward to the laboratory. Two or more specimens so packed may be placed in a larger container for shipment to the laboratory.

10. Use every precaution possible to see that the evidence reaches the laboratory in the same condition as that in which it was found. Blood, hair, fibers or other material adhering to specimens may prove of great importance to the officer in further investigation of the case.

11. Bullets imbedded in wood, etc., should be removed by cutting out a portion of the material in which the bullet lies; send the piece containing the bullet intact to the laboratory. *Do not attempt to dig a bullet out.*

12. Removal of an evidence bullet from the body of a deceased person should be done by the physician who is performing the autopsy. He should be instructed to use special care in recovering the bullet in order not to damage the delicate markings essential for laboratory identification. The recovery of such evidence bullets from wounds in a deceased person may be done by extracting the bullet with rubber-tipped forceps. *Never probe for a bullet.*

13. In all homicides, it is important that a photographic record be made of the crime scene just as it was discovered before any object in this critical area is touched or moved. The laboratory should be provided with copies of such photographs in cases where evidence is submitted for examination. In many types of cases other than homicides, photographs are helpful.
    a. If the department is not equipped to take photographs, it is suggested that a commercial photographer be called in immediately for this purpose.
    b. Using a tripod if possible, photograph the area from a sufficient distance to portray a general view of the scene and its surroundings. For room scenes, a wide-angle lens is recommended.
    c. Move the camera in closer, taking pictures from each direction until an adequate photographic record is made of the scene. Close-up photographs may be taken of objects or material of special significance.
    d. Use smallest diaphragm opening consistent with exposure conditions.
    e. Make a record of the camera position, focal length of lens, lens opening, speed and type of film used on each photograph.
    f. Include a ruler in each picture for scale purposes.
14. In addition to a photographic record, a map or diagram made to scale of the crime scene will prove of material assistance to the laboratory. In major cases, the city or county engineer can render a real service in the production of detailed diagrams.
15. The laboratory examination of powder and shot patterns on clothing may be of value in indicating the distance from which the shot was fired, and in some cases, the direction.
    a. Clothing bearing suspected powder burns or patterns in shooting cases may be prepared for transmittal to the laboratory as follows: place a clean sheet of white paper on each side of the cloth in the vicinity of the bullet holes; sandwich the cloth and paper between

two pieces of heavy cardboard; tape, seal, label, wrap and forward to the laboratory.

b. Do not attempt to cut out the suspected area; send the entire garment or garments to the laboratory.

Tool Mark Evidence

All tools bear microscopic imperfections on their cutting edges or service areas, and these defects are frequently transmitted to the object cut, hit, scraped or punched in such a manner as to permit positive identification. Tools in this class include the knife, axe, saw, hacksaw, hammer, drill, pry-bar, punch, screwdriver, pliers, chisel, bolt-cutters and others.

1. Tools submitted for examination should be prepared for shipment in a manner similar to that described for firearms evidence.

2. Do not clean, wipe or otherwise touch the cutting edge or service area of the tool.

3. Pack carefully to be sure that cutting edge or service area of tool will not come into contact with another surface while in transit. Protect it with cotton if necessary to assure this protection.

4. The imprint of the tool should be removed in whole and transmitted with the suspected tool to the laboratory. Pack in such a manner that the tool mark itself is well protected from friction or contact with any other surface or object.

Blood

1. In criminal investigation the officer often encounters stains which through laboratory analysis may yield information of considerable value in the solution of the case and in its prosecution. Perhaps the most common type of stain encountered is that of suspected blood on weapons, tools, broken glass, clothing, bed clothes, upholstery and other objects. Three principal questions usually involved in such cases are:

Can the presence of blood be established?
Is it human blood?
What type is it?

2. In many cases, all three of these questions may be answered through analysis if the evidence is properly submitted in sufficient amounts to the laboratory for examination. It is often difficult or impossible to answer questions 2 and 3 because of the small amount of evidence material submitted.

3. Do not cut out a portion of the stained area; the entire garment or article should be forwarded to the laboratory.

4. Do not ship evidence while stain is still wet. If clothing or other article bearing stain is wet or damp, allow it to air dry before packing. Do not put it in a draft and do not use either a fan or artificial heat to dry it.

5. Attach to each article of evidence a tag bearing identifying data. If there is more than one article, each must be wrapped separately in order to prevent contamination of one piece by the other. All may be placed in a larger container, sealed, labeled and forwarded to the laboratory.

6. If suspected blood stain is on upholstery, carpet, etc., saturate part of stained area with a saline solution obtained from local druggist. Press a clean blotter on the processed area to absorb part of the solution; allow the blotter to air dry; mark it with identifying data; wrap in clean white paper; place in suitable container and forward to laboratory.

Blood Stains on Solid Objects

7. Where suspected blood stains are on floor, doors or other immovable objects which cannot be sent to the laboratory, flake off particles of the dried stain with a clean knife or other instrument. If specimens are removed from different parts of a room, house, automobile, etc., use a different clean knife or other instrument for each operation. Forward the knife used for this purpose to the

laboratory with the evidence.

8. Place suspected particles from each location on a separate sheet of white paper to prevent contamination of one by the other; fold carefully, seal and label; place with other articles to be sent in a larger container and forward to the laboratory.

9. If possible, the solid object upon which these spots or stains were found should be removed, labeled and stored for trial in such a manner that the stained region will not be touched by any other surface or otherwise contaminated.

10. Where blood stains are suspected on weapons, tools, broken glass or other portable objects, the article should be sent to the laboratory intact. Use every care in preparing for shipment to prevent dislodging hairs, fibers and small particles of foreign material. These may prove more important than the suspected blood stain.

Tests for Degree of Intoxication

11. Blood alcohol determinations will be made upon fresh blood submitted to the laboratory in criminal cases. Ten cubic-centimeters of blood sealed in a clean glass container is sufficient for a determination. Blood specimen should completely fill the container to eliminate air pockets.

12. The same rules pertaining to legally admissable confessions should be observed in obtaining blood specimens from suspect.

13. The blood specimen should be taken under the supervision of a licensed physician.

14. Blood alcohol determinations may be of the greatest importance to the investigation in homicides, hit-and-run cases and fatal traffic accidents.

15. If blood is taken from a deceased person for this purpose, it *must be collected before embalming.*

Seminal Stains

1. In the investigation of rape and other sex offenses, the presence of semen stains may be a determining factor. Due to the nature of this particular type of offense, semen stains will almost always be found on clothing, blankets or other textile materials.
2. Do not cut out suspected stained area; allow it to dry if damp and send complete garment or garments.
3. Wrap each garment or article separately to avoid contamination of one by the other and label each for identification; place all articles in a larger container, seal and label for transmittal to the laboratory.
4. In rape cases, examination of the victim by a physician may be indicated for recovery of semen from the vagina. If the victim is a minor, the physician *must obtain the consent of parents or lawful guardian* before undertaking such examination. A careful search of her person should be made by the physician for foreign hairs. All clothing worn by the victim at the time of the attack should be submitted to the laboratory. In the struggle during the attack the victim may have collected valuable evidence under her fingernails.
5. The suspect should be stripped and examined for injuries, hairs in his foreskin and semen on his genitalia. Suspected garments worn by him at the time of the alleged attack should be forwarded to the laboratory.

Fingernail Scrapings

1. In homicides and other attacks against persons, including sex offenses, residue under fingernails of both victim and suspect may provide the investigator with conclusive evidence.

    In all situations where the victim has offered resistance to an attack, fingernail scrapings should be obtained from both victim and suspect. In a rape case, for example, if suspect is actually the guilty party, minute particles of skin, blood, hair and cosmetics can often be found which may possess identification value. Small fibers may be found which can be identified as having come from the victim's clothing. Likewise, the nail scrapings of the victim may yield important information.

2. Fingernail scrapings (residue from beneath fingernails) should be taken with a clean knife or other instrument and placed in small, clean, round pill boxes. Residue from each finger should be placed in a separate box, sealed, labeled and forwarded to the laboratory.

Hair

1. Hair may be involved as evidence in criminal cases under a great variety of circumstances. It may be found in the grasp of a victim, under fingernails, on his or her clothing, on weapons of attack, on bed clothing, in hats, on the radiator grill or fender of an automobile and on other objects.

2. While the identification value of hair is more limited than is the case with many other types of evidence, it may provide important corroborating information, and its value should not be overlooked in any criminal investigation.

3. Handle suspected hair specimens with clean fingers; do not use tweezers or other instruments; place hair on sheet of clean white paper; fold, seal, label and then place in an envelope or other container for forwarding to the laboratory. Do not place hair evidence in an envelope without first wrapping in a sheet of white paper as described above.

4. If hair is found on a weapon of attack (club, hammer, gun, axe etc.) and it seems to be firmly attached, leave hair intact on the weapon; label weapon and pack in such a manner that hair cannot possibly become detached or lost in transit.

5. Hair evidence should be handled in such a way that any microscopic foreign material present on the hair will not

be disturbed or lost, as this material may frequently be as valuable, or more so, than the hair itself.
6. Where hair evidence is submitted, a generous sample of known hair from victim and from suspect if in custody should accompany the evidence. Known sample should be wrapped in a separate paper but may be forwarded in the larger container with the evidence hair.

Fibers, Threads, Textiles, Twines, Cord, Rope

1. Often small fragments of textiles, threads, lint and fibers may be found by the officer adhering to weapons of attack, under fingernails of victim or suspect, on windows or other points of entry in burglary and on some other objects. Laboratory examination of this type of evidence often reveals information of importance to the investigating officer.
2. Examination of twines, cord and rope involved as evidence in a criminal case may likewise yield important information.
3. Prepare fibers and threads for transmittal to the laboratory in the same manner as that described for hair evidence.
4. Twines, cord or rope will present little difficulty in preparing for shipment.
5. Handle this type of evidence carefully to avoid disturbing soil, dusts, blood or other foreign material that may be present on fiber, thread and so forth.
6. Fragments torn from garments or other fabrics may be matched as to position and similarity.

Dusts

1. Dusts and other microscopic debris in clothing and on weapons and instruments of attack may prove of value as evidence.
2. Object bearing suspected materials should be sent to the laboratory intact for examination.

Soils

1. Laboratory examination of soils collected on shoes and car fenders may prove of value in tracing the movements of the suspect.
2. Soil may be impressed in the clothing of rape and assault victims and in the clothing of suspects; comparisons may be made with samples from the site of the attack.
3. Clothing bearing suspected soil materials should be prepared for transmittal to the laboratory by wrapping each article separately in clean paper; seal all openings with cellophane tape and label. If more than one article of clothing is being sent, wrap each separately as above indicated and place all in a larger container for shipment to the laboratory.
4. Suitable soil samples must be collected from the suspected source and submitted to the laboratory. Do not dig beneath the surface for soil sample; gather from surface of top layer. Place in clean glass jar, seal, label and forward.
5. If suspected soil materials are on an object other than clothing, such as weapons or tools, prepare for shipment as described before.
6. If object bearing suspected soil materials cannot be forwarded to the laboratory, flake off suitable samples of suspected material, place in clean glass jar just large enough to hold sample, seal, label and ship.

Metals

1. Metal traces may be found in the clothing of burglary suspects and on tools such as hammers, chisels, drills, punches, pry-bars and other instruments, which may link them with the case under investigation. The examination of wire, cable and other metallic materials may be indicated also.
2. Prepare clothing for shipment to the laboratory as outlined previously.

3. Prepare tools and other objects for transmittal as indicated previously.

Paint

1. Paint from the car involved may be left in identifiable trace amounts on the clothing of the victim in traffic accident cases and on tools used in burglaries, as well as on other objects involved in criminal investigations. The composition of a paint evidence specimen may be determined by laboratory analysis and compared with samples removed from the suspected car, or from a safe, window, transom, door and so forth.
2. Follow previous instructions for transmitting clothing to the laboratory.
3. In removing paint sample from a suspected car, it should be flaked off with a clean knife at or near the point of impact.

   Photograph that portion of car where the sample is taken. Never use the same knife to remove samples from two different sources; make a notation in your notebook that this precaution was taken.
4. Paint specimens should be placed in small, clean, round pill boxes, sealed, labeled and transmitted to the laboratory. Where paint specimens are removed from two or more different locations, the paint from each location should be placed in a separate box.
5. Tools and other instruments bearing suspected paint traces should be sent intact to the laboratory; wrap carefully to prevent loss of important evidence; follow packing instructions.

Glass

1. Headlight lens fragments recovered at the scenes of hit-and-run accidents, windshield fragments, fractured glass found at the scene of burglaries, small glass fragments left in the clothing of traffic accident victims

and burglary suspects or on tools and other instruments may yield important information under laboratory analysis.

2. In the examination of headlight lens fragments, the damaged headlight from the suspected car should be dismounted, properly packed, sealed, labeled and sent to the laboratory together with lens fragments recovered at the scene. Wrap all specimens separately in cotton to avoid further breakage; seal and label each item. All may be carefully packed in a larger container for shipment to the laboratory.

3. Suspected tools to be examined in this connection may be prepared for shipment as previously outlined.

Ash

1. In certain situations, the laboratory examination of ash residue may give positive results in the investigation of a criminal case. The destruction of incriminating evidence is sometimes attempted by burning. Combustion is frequently incomplete. Under analysis, important information may be revealed concerning the nature and source of the material burned. Charred documents may yield valuable clues for the investigator.

2. Special care is necessary in preparing ash residue for transmittal to the laboratory. Place in clean glass container of proper size. Ash residue should fill container selected for this purpose in order to immobilize contents as far as possible. Seal, label and forward to laboratory.

Drugs and Poisons

1. In suspected poisoning cases, the laboratory will examine evidence such as foods in liquid or solid form, drugs and other materials.

2. Blood alcohol determinations will be made in cases where death from excessive use of alcohol is suspected. Follow previous instructions for preparation of blood sample.

3. Blood analysis will be made for the presence of carbon monoxide. Follow instruction for preparation of blood sample.

4. In every case of suspected poisoning, make an immediate search for possible sources of the poisoning agent and container.

5. If a suspected container is found, close with tight fitting stopper or screw top, seal and label. Pack with cotton in a suitable container to avoid breakage in transit and forward immediately to the laboratory. Use every precaution to prevent leakage of any portion of the substance from the container.

6. If suspected specimen is not already in a suitable container, place in small clean glass bottle with tight-fitting stopper and prepare for transmittal as outlined above.

7. If already in a suitable container, such as a fruit jar, etc., suspected food specimens may be left in such container for shipment. If not, place in a clean glass container, seal with tight fitting lid, label and pack for shipment as above outlined.

8. The laboratory performs no autopsies. In cases where such procedure may be indicated, consult the coroner in your jurisdiction.

Restoration of Obliterated Numbers on Metal Objects Such as Firearms or Typewriters

1. Through the application of laboratory methods, it is often possible to restore stamped serial numbers which have been removed from firearms, typewriters, automobile parts and other metal objects. Restoration of such numbers may aid the investigator in tracing ownership of a suspected weapon or other article.

2. Pack weapons for transmittal to the laboratory as previously outlined.

3. Other objects, such as typewriters, automobile parts, etc.,

may be packed in a suitable box, sealed, labeled and sent to the laboratory for examination.

Bombs and Other High Explosives

Do not attempt to transport or ship bombs or other known high explosives. Clear vicinity of civilians, place area under guard and call nearest military post or telephone laboratory for instructions.

Incendiary Attacks

1. In arson cases, physical, mechanical or chemical methods may be employed for the timing of fires of incendiary origin. These include candles, kerosene and other inflammable liquids, matches, cigarettes, twines, fuses, clockwork mechanisms, sodium metal, phosphorous and others. All of these methods may leave detectable traces in the residues to be found at the scene after the fire.
2. Determine point in house or other structure at which fire originated as nearly as possible; observe any plants of inflammable material at other locations in the building to spread the fire once it is started. Carefully collect suspected materials at these points, including ash, charred fragments, mechanical devices and other items, and transmit them, properly packed, sealed and labeled, to the laboratory.

The foregoing illustrates the wide range and diversity of materials that may become involved as evidence during the investigation of a criminal case. Even a piece of string may speak with the voice of authority. The almost unbelievable story told by a short piece of string in one case led to the prompt arrest of four people who had entered into a conspiracy to take a man's life. The intended victim arose rather early one morning to look at some flowers he had planted below his bedroom window the night before. He saw in the flower bed a strange looking package. There extended from the package a piece of thick white string which was burning at one end. With rare presence of mind, he drew out his pocket knife and cut the fuse apart.

He called the police, and following their arrival, the package was taken to police headquarters for examination. The laboratory expert found that it contained ten sticks of dynamite. In addition to other phases of the examination, a laboratory analysis was made of residue recovered from a piece of brown string which held this lethal package together.

As a result of these tests, the laboratory reported to the Chief of Detectives during the afternoon of the same day that the package came from a farm on which would be found sorrel horses, Jersey cows, black-and-white rabbits, pine trees, two varieties of rare plants, Rhode Island Red chickens and a fast stream of running water. This incredible store of information extracted from a piece of string shortened the investigative trail and led to the arrest of three men and a woman who had stolen the dynamite and who were parties to this threat against a man's life.

THE POLICE LABORATORY

Every police department, regardless of size, even the smallest, should have at least a rudimentary police laboratory. Even though the equipment may be limited and no highly trained specialists present with degrees in the laboratory sciences, the smaller police department can easily and with relatively little expense develop an elementary laboratory facility that can serve very important purposes.

The nucleus of such a laboratory is a photographic darkroom and basic camera equipment. The Eastman Kodak Company and other suppliers of photographic equipment will gladly furnish a department with detailed plans for the darkroom. In order of importance, the basic elements of a simple police laboratory include the following:

1. Photographic darkroom.
2. A view camera with flash attachment.
3. Elementary lighting equipment.
4. Latent fingerprint camera.
5. Investigation kit.

The view camera is a multipurpose piece of equipment. It serves for the photography of crime and traffic accident scenes and for the "mugging" of arrested persons, when it is too early to purchase more sophisticated equipment for this purpose. Mounted on a tripod, it is also useful in photographing latent fingerprints on articles and objects that have been brought in to headquarters from the scene, and in photographing other types of evidence.

The fingerprint camera is designed primarily for field use in photographing latent impressions on objects that cannot conveniently be taken to headquarters. There are occasionally situations where the fingerprint camera cannot be used because of the contour of the surface on which the print has been developed. In such cases, the view camera can be used effectively. The author has made it a practice never to "lift" a latent fingerprint impression except as a last resort.

From the standpoint of personnel, the identification officer is usually the man in charge of laboratory work. A police officer with an enthusiastic interest in scientific crime detection and with elementary equipment can make important contributions to the investigative process. As Wilson observed, whenever he searches for, develops and photographs latent fingerprints, photographs the scenes of crimes and serious accidents, and makes casts of footprints and other impressions, he is engaged in *scientific crime detection.**

In addition to its value in the processing of evidence materials, the presence of such a laboratory facility in the smaller department cultivates a scientific attitude on the part of police personnel and sharpens the approach in the search for evidence and its care and preservation.

Where the nature of the required laboratory examination or analysis is too involved for the smaller laboratory, standing by are crime laboratories in nearby larger or metropolitan police departments, state crime laboratories and the incomparable laboratory facilities of the Federal Bureau of Investigation in Washington, D. C.

---

*Wilson, O. W.: *Police Administration.* New York, McGraw-Hill Book Company, 1950, p. 120.

V

COLLATERAL ELEMENTS
OF THE INVESTIGATIVE PROCESS

MODUS OPERANDI

MODUS OPERANDI, or operational profile of the criminal offender is one of the most important investigative tools at the disposal of the police. The system of *modus operandi* analysis was developed shortly after the turn of the century by Colonel L. S. Atcherley who was in charge of the Yorkshire West Riding Constabulary in England, and its success in that country led to its adoption by a number of American police departments.

It is based upon a conclusion, consistent with our knowledge of human behavior, that the criminal in his defensive position develops individual techniques and methods which he considers conducive to safety and success and, further, that a fairly high degree of persistence of certain factors will be found in the operating pattern of any given individual. It becomes a matter of habit, in much the same manner that a large percentage of people put on the same shoe first every morning. It may be either the left or right shoe, but it is always the same one.

Within a given criminal specialty such as burglary or worthless check operations for example, Colonel Atcherly determined through the analysis of thousands of crimes that each criminal offender followed an identifying pattern of operation in committing his crime, and that astute investigation at the scene of the crime would reveal the characteristic delineations of this pattern. He found that often the *modus operandi* or operating pattern included small, irrelevant acts which had no relationship at all to the actual commission of the crime and which could be accounted for only by the personality characteristics and general behavior pattern of the individual.

The primary elements of a criminal offender's *modus operandi*

78

are as follows:

Persons attacked. This includes the number of victims, their sex, whether adults or juveniles, race and insofar as possible, their occupations. This is important because some criminals operate against a certain sex, grown persons or juveniles, certain races, certain types of professional people, and so forth.

Property attacked. This means the type of premise in which the offense was committed. If a bank were held up, the property attacked would be a bank. In police crime reports, stores are described as to type of business and whether independent or chain. Where a building is used for a number of purposes, the purpose for which the particular room entered is used is noted, and after that the general use of the building. Some examples are a grocery store under apartment, dentist's office in front of residence or sleeping quarters in rear of grocery store. Buildings are described as to the number of families living therein and the type of building, as bungalow, apartment, club, etc.

How attacked. This refers to the way in which the person or property was attacked. In burglary, property is attacked by breaking in. The point of entry, such as rear door, first floor, side window or first-floor transom is noted. In the case of robbery, is is noted whether the victim was strong-armed, slugged, threatened, choked, beaten, shot, etc. In worthless checks, were they passed, forged or raised, or were they fictitious or fraudulent checks, drafts or notes? In larceny one must note the place from where the property was stolen, i.e. cash register, clothesline, desk, kitchen, etc.

Means of attack. This refers to the instrument, tool, device, trick or method by which the person or property was attacked. In burglary, all tools used are described briefly but specifically. In the case of robbery, the best possible description of the weapon used is given. In larceny, the means may be merely by carrying away; climbing adjoining premises or a fence, fire escape, ladder, porch, or rope; by driving away, by shoplifting or by taking with any instrument.

Time of attack. This refers to both the time reported and the actual time the offense was committed, in terms of hour of day, day of week, week of month, and month of year.

Object of attack. The objects of attack of one criminal may be money, with him overlooking other articles of real value. Others will take money and jewelry, or certain types of clothing, or silverware, etc. In crimes against the person, not involving property, the object of attack will be the motive rather than a material thing, i.e. illicit love affair or insurance plot.

Trademark. This is concerned with the personal idiosyncracies or peculiar methods of operation which may serve to distinguish the offense from other crimes committed in much the same fashion. Some men commit a robbery with no fuss and very little conversation, while others make a great deal of noise, commotion and conversation. Some men turn on house lights in a burglary, while others burn matches or use flashlights. Some invariably raid the refrigerator, whereas others will take food into the premises. A man who gains entrance to a house by representing himself as an inspector from a gas or electric company is an old type.

Such items as committed the crime during a funeral or party, assaulted the occupant while he was bathing, did malicious damage to premises, wrote obscene note with soap on a mirror in the bathroom, poisoned dog, cut telephone wires, pretended to be blind, rearranged furniture and so forth, are all examples of trademark. Many times, a trademark has nothing at all to do with the commission of the crime. The more unusual, the more queer, strange or peculiar the trademark is, the greater its value in identifying the perpetrator of future crimes or of connecting a suspect with past crimes.

On the Pacific Coast, for example, a burglar operated for a number of years all the way from Vancouver, British Columbia, to San Diego, California, before he was finally apprehended. At the scene of his crimes, he always worked in his stocking feet and came to be known by the police as "The Barefoot Burglar." His trademark was most unusual and in one city alone, this particular element in his *modus operandi* made it possible for the police to bring together one hundred and eighty-five unsolved burglary cases with the firm assurance that they had all been committed by the same individual.

After entering a home, he would apparently become quite unhappy about the way the lady of the house had arranged the furniture. In his view, the piano would look much better on the other side of the living room. The divan and easy chair, as well as other living room furnishings, were entirely out of place in their present location.

Once the living room had been rearranged to his entire satisfaction, he would proceed to other rooms in the house where he would usually be disappointed again with the arrangement of the furniture and even the pictures on the wall. In many cases, everything was rearranged, requiring something in the nature of a busy evening's work. He operated during the theatre hours and people have been known to come home from the show, unlock the door and after one glance inside, come back out and look at the house number to be sure they were in the right place.

He would do all of these things before getting down to the business at hand — that of stealing money, jewelry and clothing. Like all criminals, he finally made the fatal mistake: he was apprehended one evening when he failed to exercise enough discrimination in the choice of the next scene for his operations — a home in Santa Barbara, California, where an off-duty policeman was in bed asleep.

Modus operandi actually cleared a series of nineteen murders extending all the way from Lake Coeur d'Alene in the state of Idaho to southern California. The victims were all women. Mr. W. would in every case insert an advertisement in the classified section of a newspaper in the "Personal" column, reading somewhat as follows: "Cultured, middle-aged gentleman of means would like to make the acquaintance of refined lady of similar background, object matrimony. Write Box 742 in care of this newspaper."

As the replies came in, he would scan his mail carefully and select a letter that struck his fancy. There would be a telephone call to complete arrangements for their first meeting. Then would follow a whirl-wind courtship. Although the man was not at all attractive — about 5′ 6″ in height; a thin, scrawny, jaundiced face; eyes sunk back in their sockets, hollow cheeks, partially bald and about forty-five years of age — he seemed to have a way with women.

Then, as on Lake Coeur d'Alene, while they were walking along the shore one moonlight evening, he suddenly picked up a rock and crushed her skull. He must have liked lakes, for on Lake Washington in Seattle one evening in a canoe with the next victim, he asked her to stand up in the boat. He then rocked the canoe until she lost her balance and fell into the water. She was a good swimmer, but every time she came near enough to catch hold of the boat, he would hit her over the head with an oar. Actually, some of the details of his *modus operandi* were too hideous and revolting to be printed in a book. He was a sadist.

The time element in the *modus operandi* — the hour of the day the crime was committed, the day of the week, the week of the month, the month of the year and even the season may mark the turning point in a criminal investigation.

In a western city, the police had been plagued by a series of burglaries extending over a period of several years. The burglar would always enter a vacant store and cut a hole in the wall for entry into the store next door. This was but one of several factors in his *modus operandi* that led the police to conclude that one man was responsible for some eighty-five burglaries.

What is called a composite *modus operandi* analysis was made of all eighty-five cases. When the study was completed, one thing stood out like the beam from a lighthouse on a dark night. All of the burglaries had been committed during a particular three months of the year — December, January and February. During the other nine months of the year, he was evidently out of the city for some reason, since no burglary reports were received during this period by the police showing the same method of operation.

The police then cast about to find an occupation that would take a man out of the city all year except for the months of December, January and February. They found it — a company that operated a fleet out of San Francisco up on the fishing banks near Alaska. Police investigators then examined the payroll records of this company for the names of employees who lived in or near the city in question.

Out of four men on the payroll who resided in the vicinity, the police found one who had served a sentence in prison and his fingerprints were therefore on file in the police records division. They were compared with latent fingerprint impressions developed on milk bottles — he always opened the refrigerator on the job, another characteristic of his method of operation. A positive identification was made, and a police reception committee awaited him on the occasion of his next return to the city. He chose to fight it out in a gun battle with the officers and came out second best.

In the course of the investigation that followed, it was found that he had stolen the sand and cement that went into the foundation of the home that he had built. All of the lumber in the house was stolen as well as the doors and windows, the living room furnishings, furniture in the bedrooms, kitchen stove, refrigerator — everything from the basement to the roof had been stolen. Behind the walls and underneath the floor boards, loot was found including a variety of items all the way from canned tomatoes to diamond rings and wrist watches.

In cases without number, investigating officers can determine who they are looking for through a careful study of the *modus operandi* at the scene of the crime. In Scotland Yard, the *modus operandi* system is used on a very extensive scale. In that noted organization, the *modus operandi* section of the training manual used for training personnel is called "Catching Thieves on Paper."

In the United States, an increasing number of police departments are making effective use of the *modus operandi* system. In the larger departments, on all theft cases reported to the police — robbery, burglary, larceny, worthless checks and automobile theft — the elements of the *modus operandi* in each case is punched on tabulating code cards and placed on file. A *modus operandi* search of thousands of these cards requires only a few minutes.

The *modus operandi* in an uncleared burglary case, for example, is coded and programmed on the automatic sorting machine. *Modus operandi* cards on file are then run through the sorting machine and all cases with the same or similar *modi operandi* are automatically selected. The operation serves two investigative purposes:

1. On uncleared cases, it brings together offense reports with the same or similar *modi operandi,* with the probability that all or most of these cases were committed by the same individual.
2. By running through the automatic sorting machine cases cleared in the past with the same or similar *modi operandi* as currently unsolved cases, it may indicate to the police who they are looking for.

Metropolitan and state police computer installations offer unlimited opportunities in the *modus operandi* identification of a crime series and the identification of criminal offenders. Through the use of the computer, the verdict is virtually instantaneous.

In the smaller police departments, the same operation can be conducted effectively through the use of index cards. Through cross-index classification, the *modus operandi* or method of operation on each case of theft can be broken down and factored into its component parts as an investigative aid in the identification of a crime series and as an aid in the identification of the offender. These cross-index divisions are:

1. Crime classification.
2. Where committed (location index, spot maps, etc.).
3. Time of attack.
4. Person or property attacked.
5. How attacked.
6. Means of attack.
7. Object of attack.
8. Trademark.

Each main index division will have a number of subdivisions. Time of attack, for instance, would be broken down by hour of day, day of week, week of month and month of year. As these index files build up, and through cross-indexing and searching in the *modus operandi* file of current cases reported to the police for investigation, important identifications can be made, with an increase in the quantity and quality of departmental performance.

How the persistance of the *modus operandi* pattern in the operations of the individual criminal offender can be effectively exploited is illustrated in the following example. A department had experienced a series of twenty-eight burglaries over a period of three months. Fifteen of these burglaries were committed by a thief who used matches instead of a flashlight and always drank milk from the refrigerator during his nocturnal raids. These traits linked all fifteen cases, but the officers still lacked any description of the suspect. A search of the *modus operandi* files pointed to three different burglars with a similar pattern of operation. It was learned by the officers that two were then in prison. The third had just been released on parole. Parole records revealed his address and a speedy clearance of fifteen burglary cases followed.

INTERROGATION

In the general administration of criminal justice, information at the investigative stage in a criminal case is the most vital element in the total process. Sources of information available to the police and their wide range and diversity have been previously considered. However, the greatest volume of direct information bearing upon guilt or innocence is obtained through the interrogation of criminal suspects and through interviewing witnesses and others who may possess relevant information concerning the case under investigation.

The line of distinction between an interview and an interrogation is very thin. Both involve questioning and more important, listening. An interview can be regarded as a formal consultation with a person who may have knowledge that is of official interest to the investigating officer. On the other hand, an interrogation is the systematic questioning of a criminal suspect or of a person who is reluctant to disclose information in his possession which is pertinent to the investigation.

Much has been written concerning the techniques of interrogation, and it would be idle to involve the reader in any detailed discussion of the subject at this point. Since interrogation is one of the most important investigative tools at the disposal of the police, every police officer should spend much time and effort in studying the works in this area that are now available. Some of these are

1. O'Hara, Charles E.: *Fundamentals of Criminal Investigation.* Springfield, Thomas, 1956, pp. 79-94, 95-114.
2. Inbau and Reed: *Lie Detection and Criminal Interrogation.*

Baltimore, Williams & Wilkins, 1953.
3. Vanderbosch, Charles G.: *Criminal Investigation.* International Association of Chiefs of Police, 1968, pp. 196-209.
4. Dudycha, George J.: *Psychology for Law Enforcement Officers.* Springfield, Thomas, 1955.
5. Clift, Raymond E.: *A Guide to Modern Police Thinking,* 2nd ed. Cincinnati, W. H. Anderson, 1965, pp. 132-143.
6. Grace, Richard C., Coffey, Alan, and Eldefonso, Edward: *Principles of Law Enforcement.* New York, John Wiley, 1968, pp. 215-217.
7. Gerber, Samuel R., and Schroeder, Oliver, Jr., *Criminal Investigation and Interrogation.* W. H. Anderson, 1962, pp. 247-306.

In the interrogation of a criminal suspect, it is well to keep in mind that the suspect labors under a psychological compulsion to tell everything that he knows. As the eminent authority on evidence, John Henry Wigmore, observed:

In the first place, an innocent person is always helped by an early opportunity to tell his whole story; hundreds of suspected persons every day are set free because their story thus told bears the marks of truth. Moreover, and more important, every guilty person is almost always ready and desirous to confess as soon as he is detected and arrested. This psychological truth, well known to all criminal trial judges, seems to be ignored by some Supreme Courts.

The nervous pressure of guilt is enormous; the load of the deed done is heavy; the fear of detection fills the consciousness; and when detection comes, the pressure is relieved, and the deep sense of relief makes confession a satisfaction. At that moment, he will tell, and tell it truly. To forbid soliciting him, to seek to prevent this relief is to fly in the face of nature.*

It is natural and should be lawful to take his confession at that moment — the best one. And this expedient saves the State a delay and expense in convicting him after he has reacted from his first sensations, has yielded to his friends'

*Professor Wigmore is here referring to restrictions placed by the United States Supreme Court on the police interrogation of criminal suspects.

solicitations and comes the sway of the natural human instinct to struggle to save himself by the aid of all technicalities.

In the case of professional criminals who usually work in groups, there is often no hope of getting at the group until one of them has "preached" and given the clues to the police. The police know this and have known it for generations in every country. The only ones who apparently do not know it are some of the Supreme Court judges . . . . To forbid this (interrogation) is to tie the hands of the police. The attitude of some judges towards these necessary police methods is lamentable . . . . To disable the police from the very function they are set to fulfill is no less than absurd. Let the judges who sit in judgment on crime look a little into the facts. Let them not sit up aloft and dictate a rule which ignores the well-known facts of criminal life and hampers the needful methods of justice.*

Legal Aspects of Interrogation

The United States Supreme Court has placed certain restrictions on the interrogation of a criminal suspect in custody which must be observed by the investigating officer. Under the law as it stands today, the prosecution may not use statements to exonerate or convict, stemming from custodial interrogation of the defendant, unless it demonstrates procedural safeguards to secure the privilege against self-incrimination.

In the noted case, *Miranda v. Arizona,*† the Court spelled out in unmistakable detail the procedures that must be followed by the police as they approach the interrogation of a criminal suspect. In the words of Mr. Chief Justice Warren,

> Our holding will be spelled out with some specificity in the pages which follow, but briefly stated it is this: the prosecution may not use statements, whether exculpatory or inculpatory, stemming from the custodial interrogation of the defendant, unless it demonstrates the use of procedural

---

*Wigmore, John Henry: *Evidence in Trials at Common Law.* 3rd ed., Boston, Little, 1940, vol. 3, 851 at 319.
†Miranda v. Arizona, 384 U. S. 436 (1966).

safeguards to secure the privilege against self-incrimination. By custodial interrogation, we mean questioning initiated by law enforcement officers after a person has been taken into custody or otherwise deprived of his freedom of action in any significant way. As for the procedural safeguards to be employed, *unless other fully effective means are devised to inform accused persons of their right of silence and to assure a continuous opportunity to exercise it, the following measures are required: Prior to any questioning, the person must be warned that he has the right to remain silent, that any statement he does make may be used as evidence against him and that he has a right to the presence of an attorney, either retained or appointed.* The defendant may waive effectuation of these rights, provided the waiver is made voluntarily, knowingly and intelligently. *If, however, he indicates in any manner and at any stage of the process that he wishes to consult with an attorney before speaking, there can be no questioning. Likewise, if the individual is alone and indicates in any manner that he does not wish to be interrogated, the police may not interrogate him.* The mere fact that he may have answered some statements on his own does not deprive him of the right to refrain from answering any further inquiries until he has consulted with an attorney and thereafter consents to be questioned.

It is now mandatory on the part of the police that they observe the following instructions of the Court before the custodial interrogation of a suspect begins:

1. At the outset, if a persons in custody is to be subjected to interrogation, he must first be informed in clear and unequivocal terms that he has the right to remain silent.
2. The warning of the right to remain silent must be accompanied by the explanation that anything he says can and will be used against him in court.
3. An individual held for interrogation must be clearly informed that he has the right to consult with a lawyer and to have the lawyer with him during the interrogation.
4. It is necessary to warn him not only that he has the right to consult with an attorney but also that if he is indigent, a lawyer will be appointed to represent him.

Police Use of the Polygraph

As an aid to interrogation, the polygraph or lie detector is now standard equipment in most American police departments in cities of 50,000 and above. As early as 1959, a survey revealed that police departments in more than two hundred American cities and the State Police in forty-eight states were making use of the polygraph.* The survey further indicated the extent to which the polygraph is being employed in the armed forces, including the United States Air Force, the Marines and the Military Police. The polygraph training program at the Provost Marshal General's School at Camp Gordon, Georgia, is conceded to be among the best and most comprehensive programs of this type in the entire United States.

Much greater use of the polygraph should be made in the smaller police departments of the nation. In departments with a personnel strength of from thirty to seventy-five officers, the presence of a polygraph and a trained polygraph examiner would seem be mandatory. The investment in the instrument and in the training of an examiner would yield handsome dividends.

While university training in psychology, physiology and the other behavior sciences is very desirable, it is not altogether absolutely indispensable. However, it is strongly recommended. There are at least two schools in the United States where adequate polygraph training may be obtained — the Keeler Polygraph Institute in Chicago, and Backster's Lie Detection Training Center in New York City.

Police departments with a personnel strength under thirty officers should no longer hesitate to take their suspects in important criminal cases to nearby larger departments where the services of a trained and competent polygraph examiner would be available.

For more than forty years, the polygraph has proven its worth to the police in declaring the innocent and exposing the guilt of the criminal offender. As an aid to interrogation in the early stages of case investigation, it has shortened the investigative trail to a point where from an economic point of view and increased police

---

*Gootnick, Louis, *A Survey of Police Use of the Polygraph,* Master's Thesis, New York University, October, 1959.

efficiency, there should be no further delay in extending the police use of this important facility. Some departments follow the policy of examining on the polygraph virtually all persons arrested, including those in the "suspicious character" category. Where this policy is followed, the number of uncleared criminal cases in the files of the department is materially reduced.

The use of the polygraph is also now well established in the screening of police applicants. It has proven to be effective in discouraging patently unqualified candidates from even applying for a position in the department. In addition, there is its obvious value in disclosing important information unreported on the application form, such as prior criminal involvement in unreported or unsolved crimes, abnormal sexual tendencies and other unfavorable information.

The conservative *Wall Street Journal** featured on the front page of its October, 1961, issue an article on the expanding use of the polygraph by business and industry in the screening of personnel. On the roster of known users of the polygraph were major companies in steel production, copper refining, automobile manufacturing, meat packing, food processing, oil refining, electronics manufacturing, mail order retailing and wholesale drug concerns. Lloyd's of London recognizes the worth of the polygraph by granting insurance premium reductions on embezzlement and other forms of theft where the company or business in question processes its personnel periodically on the polygraph.

Inventory shrinkage across the nation is big business, amounting to a total annual loss nationally of between one and a half and two billion dollars. The director of security for one wholesale drug concern, who is a trained polygraph examiner, observed that at the time he became associated with the company, they were experiencing an annual inventory shrinkage of between three and four million dollars. It is estimated by security personnel that of every ten dollars loss, one dollar may be attributed to shoplifting and other forms of outside theft, and nine dollars to employee or employee-related theft. The important role of the polygraph and

---

*Leonard, V. A.: *Police Organization and Management,* 2nd ed. Santa Ana, Foundation Press, 1964, p. 224.

its associated techniques in the approach to this problem is thus self-evident.

In some states, attempts have been made to pass legislation prohibiting the use of the polygraph in the screening of personnel on the grounds that it invaded the privacy and rights of the individual. This is totally unacceptable. The polygraph examination performs exactly the same function as the application form and background investigation in revealing information concerning the applicant to a prospective employer. No objection to the application form and background investigation has as yet been heard. As a former president of the Academy for Scientific Interrogation, a national organization of polygraph examiners, the author is of the opinion that the motives of persons interested in this type of legislation should be carefully examined.

The polygraph is a diagnostic instrument and functions as an instrumental aid in the diagnosis of truth or deception. The technical aspects of the polygraph examination and the interpretation of the results require the presence of a well-trained and experienced examiner. This is no place for the novice or amateur. There is a definite trend among the states toward a qualifying State Board Examination and the licensing of polygraph examiners. Kentucky in 1962 was the first to take this desirable step with Senate Bill No. 63, and similar bills have been under consideration by legislatures in other states, including New York, Illinois, Wisconsin and California.

Research directed toward further improvements in instrumental design and examination techniques continues apace. Much of this research, and that is considerable, is being undertaken by medical schools and their Departments of Psychiatry throughout the country, in connection with the study of the emotions.

ADMINISTRATIVE ALTERNATIVES

One bright spot on the horizon in connection with the availability of the services of a polygraph examiner to the smaller police forces is a growing trend toward the merger of police operations on an area basis. Among the results of such consolidations are increased financial capability, increased purchasing power and increased personnel resources.

Four administrative alternatives to the conventional police department have appeared on the scene, and they have proven of interest to the police and other officials in the smaller communities and cities of this country. They are:

1. The metropolitan police authority.
2. The federated police system.
3. Integrated fire and police services.
4. Contract law enforcement.

The Metropolitan Police Authority

It is frequently the case that responsibility for the delivery of police service in large metropolitan areas is fragmented among a constellation of local law enforcement agencies, each operating in its own orbit and in a state of almost complete independence. There is little opportunity or incentive for operational planning on an area basis. In some instances, a system of informal cooperation has developed in a futile attempt to meet the problem.

As an alternative, and in terms of metro-planning, it has been suggested that a single metropolitan police authority be created to discharge the law enforcement function on an areawide basis, replacing the plurality of local police departments. Admittedly, this would serve a number of constructive purposes, including a unified organization, a centralized police communications system, uniform police service throughout the area, amplified police training facilities, a centralized police records system, continuity of policy, and added financial capacity and administrative capability. It is entirely possible that the American flair for local autonomy can be adjusted to accommodate this form of approach and the advantages it appears to offer.

The Federated Police System

The continued existence of a multiplied number of semi-autonomous law enforcement agencies in a single metropolitan area would seem to be incompatible with any reasonable concept of efficient police organization and administration. A federated system of police protection may prove to be an acceptable alternative. Under this arrangement, a metropolitan police agency would join with local departments in an integrated operation designed to possess the advantages of a single metropolitan police authority and yet not do violence to the principle of local autonomy.

The metropolitan agency would be responsible for certain staff services needlessly duplicated at considerable cost to the taxpayer among the various local jurisdictions. These would include a centralized police communications system, centralized police training and crime detection laboratory facilities, and a centralized police records system. This arrangement would afford an appropriate vehicle for areawide planning and operation in criminal emergency situations. It should also prove effective in carrying out certain line functions, including the control of arterial traffic. Decentralized routine patrol operations, municipal traffic regulation and control, together with certain other functions, would remain a responsibility of local departments.

Examples of a merger of police operations under one form or another and the opportunity it affords for a more economical and efficient police service include metropolitan Dade County in Florida, metropolitan Nashville-Davidson County in Tennessee and the metropolitan Toronto Police Department in Ontario. As an illustration, the metropolitan Toronto Police Department provides police protection for the entire Toronto metropolitan area, which includes 241 square miles, nearly 2 million people and 13 incorporated municipalities, including the city of Toronto. There are no independent policing agencies in metropolitan Toronto.

Integrated Fire and Police Services

Another type of merger of police operations involves the integration of police and fire services into one department — the Department of Public Safety. In the 1960's, more than seventy-three cities — forty-four in the United States and twenty-nine in Canada — were operating under an integrated police and fire system in one form or another. Up to the present time at least, integration has been confined to the small and medium-sized cities and communities. Proposals for additional police-fire mergers are in various stages of study and development in a substantial number of other communities.

Police and fire protection are usually the two largest items in municipal budgets outside of the retirement of bonded indebtedness, and the resulting economies of integration have attracted the interest of taxpayers and public officials alike.

In Sunnyvale, California, which has had a combined department, the Department of Public Safety, since 1957, the City Manager estimated that the unification of the two forces was saving the city more than $300,000 per year in comparison to what it would cost to maintain two separate departments. Although most of this saving comes from greater efficiency in the use of manpower, some of it is the result of not having to maintain two communication systems, two sets of buildings and two records facilities, as well as freedom from the duplication of other services.

Contract Law Enforcement

A fourth form of merger is contract law enforcement, a new development in recent years. Under this arrangement, a municipality dissolves its local police force and enters into a contractual relationship with the county or state for the total delivery of police service.

In Los Angeles County, for example, the Los Angeles County Sheriff's Department is operating under contracts with twenty-seven incorporated towns and cities within the county to perform all of the law enforcement functions of a police organization. Allocated to the twenty-seven communities were a minimum of eighty-five radio patrol car units, consisting of thirty-two on the day shift, thirty-three on the evening shift and twenty on the early morning shift. Contract law enforcement appears to offer the following distinct advantages:

1. *Economy.* Police service is delivered at a lower cost than would be the case where the community maintains its own police force.
2. *Professionally trained personnel on the job.*

3. *Immediate availability of emergency reenforcements at no additional costs.* This permits a city or community to pay for only the minimum necessary level of protection, while having the advantages of necessary emergency strength being available.
4. *Unbiased, nonpartisan service.* People who might have sufficient political influence to obtain special favors from a local police force are unable to obtain them from the sheriff's personnel. There is complete freedom from local pressures and local ties.

Equally deserving of attention is the trend toward consolidation of city and county governments, which would bring to an end the needless duplication of services, facilities and costs. All of the foregoing administrative alternatives to the conventional police department move the police into a prime position to provide centralized polygraphic services throughout the area policed.

As a part of professional growth in the American police field, the consolidation or merger of police operations on an area basis can be expected to continue on an accelerated scale. All of the evidence points in that direction. The taxpayer and his representatives in local government are becoming more and more aware of the reduction in public expenditures that result from curtailing the duplication of facilities and costs through merger and consolidation.

THE INVESTIGATIVE PROCESS AND THE COMPUTER

The appearance of the computer and its related technology promises a new day in accelerating the investigation of criminal cases. Through the communication channels of the telephone, radio and the teletypewriter, it brings investigating officers in the smaller communities into almost instantaneous contact with unlimited resources in the management of information concerning wanted persons, stolen property — including guns, license plates and securities — and other matters of direct investigative interest to the police.

The complexity of police problems and the volume of data to be accommodated are now reaching the point where the human factor is being challenged, and recognition must now be given to the gear of technology. It is already apparent that developments in electronic data processing are beginning to have far-reaching consequences in the American police field. The fantastic ability of electronic data processing and its brainchild, the computer, to store enormous amounts of data with split-second retrieval has prompted police administrators to extend their vision concerning the use of this sophisticated equipment in law-enforcement operations.

Today, the volume of police-oriented data is exceeding the capacity of manually operated information storage and retrieval facilities. Electronic data processing is now making available, on a technologically feasible and acceptable cost basis, information storage facilities of sufficient capacity and magnitude to foster the centralization of police records operations at the state level and on a statewide basis. The larger metropolitan departments will probably continue to maintain their own supplementary computing and storage equipment, but this would not limit their participation in the statewide system.

In reviewing the need for a new system of information management, California police officials recognized, for example, that the major problems in law enforcement records and communications are directly connected with field operations. Patrol officers of individual municipal police departments, sheriff's deputies and officers of the California Highway Patrol constantly require information on wants for specific persons, both criminal and noncriminal; information on stolen vehicles, warrants for the arrest of traffic violators and more serious offenders, identification data on suspicious automobiles and persons encountered in the field, descriptions of stolen property and records of known criminals.

Under conventional procedure, a police officer in a smaller community had to make four separate telephone calls to check out a single suspect. This included contact with the Los Angeles County Sheriff's Office, the Los Angeles Police Department and the California Highway Patrol. Even then, he could not be sure of complete, up-to-date information because of the time lag in processing reports of new offenses, new reports of stolen property, and new wants and warrants.

In outlining operational needs, California officials recognized three general categories of problems. First priority was assigned to the field check from patrol officers out on duty. This is clearly an on-line operation with immediate response-time needs.

The second group of problems concerned the follow-up investigation. Here the officer is interested in the crime reports themselves, detailed criminal records and arrest reports, *modus operandi* information, stolen property data and other information required by the officer. The third category of problems was concerned with the command and management functions of the individual department and the statutory requirements for local reporting to state government.

The California State Computer System

The California information system represents a federation of organizational computer centers. The system makes use of computers belonging to the various agencies in California involved in the administration of criminal justice. It is coordinated by the state's central information center which serves as a central electronic index and directory of information stored in the files of the participating computer centers. It functions as a switching facility.

Current information storage included a firearms file with over 2.6 million records of concealable weapons with daily inquiries numbering 100; law enforcement statistics including arrests and dispositions with 4,000 inquiries per week; narcotic prescriptions by doctor, quantity, patient, type with 30,000 inquiries per month.*

Also included in the California system is IBM equipment operated by the California Highway Patrol, which provides a rapid communication system for recording and disseminating information on stolen and wanted vehicles. Referred to as the Automatic Statewide Auto Theft Inquiry System, the IBM installation automatically records data fed to it from any one of thirty-six terminal locations. These include eight California Highway Patrol offices, twenty-four police departments in

---

*Germann, A. C., Day, Frank D., and Gallati, Robert J.: *Introduction to Law Enforcement and Criminal Justice.* Springfield, Thomas, 1968, p. 283.

California and four Nevada police departments, serving altogether more than two hundred police agencies.

To obtain information stored in the computer, a local law enforcement agency simply queries the computer by teletypewriter. Using a coded format, the license or vehicle identification is typed on a keyboard into the terminal equipment; within one second, the computer responds with all the information on file.

The New York State Identification and Intelligence System

On June 14, 1965, Governor Rockefeller signed the bill creating the New York State Identification and Intelligence System. The system is authorized to collect, coordinate, store, process, retrieve and disseminate information concerning the investigation and prosecution of crime and the general administration of criminal justice. It is designed to bring to some 3,600 agencies of criminal justice — the police, prosecutors, courts, probation, corrections and parole — the miracle of computer science and technology. What this is going to mean to the smaller police departments of the state challenges the imagination.

Local Police Computer Installations

A number of local police computer installations have been developed, including Alameda County, California; Los Angeles County, California; Boston, Massachusetts; Chicago, Illinois; Detroit, Michigan; Kansas City, Missouri; Los Angeles, California; New York City, New York; Philadelphia, Pennsylvania, and St. Louis, Missouri.

State and local police computer installations already operational provide the foundation for a nationwide criminal information system. Always keeping pace with technological developments, the Federal Bureau of Investigation has mounted a computer-based National Information Center at FBI headquarters in Washington, D. C.

The National Crime Information Center

Today, the National Crime Information Center (NCIC) is

operational and capable of furnishing needed information concerning crime and criminals in a matter of seconds, so that the officer on the street, in communities small and large, now has a wealth of information at his command at all times. The officer out on patrol and the detective, as well, can now make inquiry of stored police information and get a "real time" i.e. up-to-the-minute answer in a matter of seconds.

Records data now in storage at the National Crime Information Center include facts on stolen vehicles, vehicles used in the commission of felonies, stolen or missing license plates when all plates issued for a specific vehicle are missing, stolen guns, other items of stolen property which are serially identifiable, and wanted persons. The latter category includes all Federal fugitives and individuals wanted on local felony or misdemeanor charges where the municipality or state involved will extradite from any point in the United States. Transactions with the NCIC computer through entries and inquiries are now more than ten thousand a day.

Response times by the NCIC computer to date have more than exceeded expectations. Responses are averaging less than fifteen seconds from the time the last character of the incoming message is received until the first character of the reply is on the way back to the transmitting terminal. In case after case, it has been demonstrated that an inquiry from the street by an officer over radio or telephone to a dispatcher at an NCIC terminal can be answered back to the street in 90 seconds!

The Ultimate User

The ultimate user of this fantastic system is the patrol officer in the field. This is well illustrated in the actions of an alert Maryland State Police Officer. While on patrol on a Maryland highway, the officer noticed a vehicle parked on the shoulder of the highway. Within a mile, the officer observed two youths walking along the highway.

After sending through an inquiry to NCIC over his car radio through the Maryland State Police control terminal, he approached the two youths and questioned them concerning their identity and their reasons for being in the area. During the interrogation, the officer received a radio reply from NCIC identifying the vehicle as a stolen car, giving a complete description of the car and the date of the theft.

The elapsed time from his initial inquiry to receipt of the message was *three minutes.* The officer took the youths back to Maryland State Police Troop Headquarters where they immediately confessed the theft.

The significance of these portentious developments for the smaller police departments of this country, as the computer joins ranks with the Police Communication system, stirs the imagination — bringing as they do, to the individual patrol officer in the field, the total resources of a national criminal data bank — *and in a matter of seconds.* What a far cry from the complete isolation of the individual patrolman on his beat not too many years ago to the computerized National Crime Information Center!

INVESTIGATION RECORDS AND REPORT WRITING

The records system is the mainspring of a police organization. Its key importance in the planning and control of police operations is such that the author has written a separate book* covering police records organization and management in the smaller department.

Accurate and complete information must be available to the chief and his personnel concerning the problems that confront the department. In no other way can the police enterprise meet with any measure of success in carrying out its duties and responsibilities. Crime, delinquency, vice and traffic problems are not confined to the textbooks. They are realistic and often grisly things that rear their heads every day as a threat to the security and safety of the community.

The police must have the facts concerning these problems; and this makes mandatory a police records system that will produce the facts, and equally important, it is also concerned with how to use them in bringing the power of the force into effective contact with these problems.

---

*Leonard, V. A., *The Police Records System,* Springfield, Thomas, 1970.

The required personnel strength of a police department can be supported in the councils of local government when the facts are known and analyzed. The proper distribution of the force by function, area and time is vital to the success of the police enterprise, and this can be determined with the aid of records data from an effective police records system.

An adequate police records facility makes possible effective control over offenses committed and their investigation. Among other things, as previously noted, it expedites the apprehension of criminal offenders through a study of their *modus operandi,* the effective analysis of traffic accidents, the selection of the best men for particular assignments and for promotion and the detection of unusual problems and emerging situations.

Furthermore, through projecting the crime, vice and traffic experience of yesterday and today into tomorrow, administrative predictions can be made concerning what and how much is going to happen, and when and where. With this kind of information, the force can be deployed on a sound and rational basis.

Master Case Report

The basic element of the police records system is the master case report, referred to in some departments as the offense report or complaint report. The offense report is for the original entry of the facts concerning a criminal offense that has been brought to the department's attention. It serves as the first formal record of the offense and as the fundamental basis for headquarters' control over the investigation.

The offense or complaint report provides for the original recording of facts concerning a crime reported to the department, but if records procedure should terminate at that point, the means for control over the case investigation would still be missing.

The preparation of intelligent reports covering the investigation of a case is one of the major responsibilities of the investigating officer. Through the requirement that the officer promptly file a written report covering the results of his investigation, the means for control is established. The report is prepared by the officer assigned to the case. It may also be used by other officers who have occasion to record certain facts concerning the case in addition to those appearing on the original offense report.

Supplementary Investigation Reports

It follows that there may be several supplementary investigating reports concerning a single offense pending final disposition of the case, and that these may fall under one or more of the following categories:

1. Statements by the investigating officer on the progress of the case. These should be submitted at regular intervals while the case is under investigation and pending its final disposition.

2. Statement by the investigating officer that the report of the offense appears to be unfounded. A case should not be declared unfounded until this conclusion is approved by the commanding officer.

3. When the investigating officer has not been able to make substantial progress and recommends that the case be declared "inactive" (not cleared). In such event, the recommendation should carry the approval of the commanding officer. A case, therefore, remains open until the command-officer countersigns the officer's recommendation that it be declared inactive, or until the case is closed by actual final disposition, such as arrest of the offender or recovery of property. In this manner, active investigation is not discontinued without a review of the case by the commanding officer in charge. The investigating officer should be required to state fully his reasons for dropping the case. A large number of cases declared inactive would not be a desirable entry in an officer's performance and personnel record.

4. When additional facts concerning the case come to the attention of the investigating officer or any other member of the department.

Form of the Report

Report writing is an art and one that is essential to the orderly and prompt conduct of police business. Some officers write more fluently than others, and for them, the preparation of an investigation report presents no problem. Other officers find the writing of a report to be somewhat difficult at times. It can be said, however, that any officer, with some thought and practice, can develop a proficiency in the writing of a report that will convert the task into a pleasant experience.*

If at all possible, the report should be typewritten. The heading of the report calls for the name of the victim in the upper left-hand corner; in the center, the date the case was reported to the department for investigation, and in the upper right-hand corner, the case number.

The body of the investigation report is introduced with a brief resume which will permit the reader to determine in a general way the subject matter of the report by reading the first sentence. New writers invariably follow this pattern. An inspection of any article in a newspaper will show that in most instances the entire story is told in the first sentence.

The introduction is followed by a detailed account in narrative form of everything that the investigating officer did or learned about the case that he has not reported at some previous time. This information is to be presented clearly and concisely, and in sufficient detail so that the report explains exactly what has happened, what has been done and what has been learned. An investigation report which must be supplemented by a verbal explanation has not been properly written.

Careful attention must be given to the spelling of names and the recording of sex, color and marital status so far as it affects the name. The given name by which a person is known and initial is considered sufficient except in the case of common names such as Smith or Jones. In such instances, the full name should be given.

This part of the report includes facts as observed by the investigating officer, facts as reported to him by witnesses, and in some instances, the opinions of citizens whom the officer may have interviewed in connection with the case.

---

*See Hazelet, John C.: *Police Report Writing;* Dienstein, William; *How to Write a Narrative Investigation Report;* and Gammage, Allen Z.: *Basic Police Report Writing,* all published by Charles C Thomas, Springfield, Illinois. These books should be in every departmental library.

Description of Property

More often than not, it also includes descriptions of property, and it is here that complete accuracy is essential. Property description includes the following:

1. Name of the article.
2. Trade name.
3. Material.
4. Form.
5. Physical measurement.
6. Sensory description.
7. Design.
8. Identifying marks (letters, monograms, serial numbers, etc).
9. Value.
   a. Cost.
   b. Present value.

The property index is one of the most important of all files in the police records unit or division. All police departments will certify that it has solved many a criminal case. If used only for checking against articles sold at pawnshops, secondhand dealers and other fences, it will have earned a permanent place in any police records system.

This file should include cross-index facilities for all property reported stolen, lost or found. The serial number of all articles bearing such numbers serves as the first classification under that particular type of article. In case serial numbers are not obtainable from complainants, the cards are filed by the make or maker's name or by other identifying marks or monograms. Musical instruments, watches, cameras, tools, typewriters, bicycles, and most mechanical contrivances bear serial numbers. Initials, monograms and other special marks serve as additional index divisions.

Diamond-set articles, except rings (if marked), are filed according to the number of diamonds and next according to design. Other stone-set pieces are filed first according to type (for example, an emerald ring or diamond ring); next by design (as Tiffany, Belcher, Gypsy, etc.); and finally by size of stone. Clothing is classified as male or female, then by type of article, next by color, then by maker's name. Even though articles may carry serial numbers, they should also be indexed by other distinguishing features such as monograms, make, design or special marks.

Description of Persons

The description of persons is a key investigative tool and the greatest of care should be exercised in obtaining the original information and recording it accurately in the investigation report. A personal description includes the following:

1. Name.
2. Alias or aliases.
3. Nickname.
4. Sex.
5. Color, including race.
6. Age.
7. Height.
8. Weight.
9. Build.
10. Hair color.
11. Eye color.
12. Complexion.
13. Occupation.
14. Nativity.
15. Beard.
16. Dress.
17. Identifying marks (scars, tatoo, etc.)

Additional descriptive factors which could easily mark the difference between success and failure in the investigation of a criminal case include Social Security number, military serial number, present and former addresses, significant physical habits, manner of walk, voice, speech, personal habits, relatives and associates, posture and any bodily peculiarities.

The investigation report should include a description of the *modus operandi* of the offender whenever this can be developed. The investigation report closes with the conclusions and recommendations of the investigating officer. The end of the report is marked by the date, hour of writing and the signature of the officer.

Follow-up Reports

If the complaint or incident reported to the department for investigation is not fully disposed of as a result of the preliminary investigation and the submission by the officer of the preliminary report, he is required to make subsequent follow-up reports covering his continued investigation of the case on follow-up report form blanks provided for this purpose. It should be an inviolable rule that follow-up reports are to be submitted on all open cases within three days following the date of the preliminary report and weekly thereafter until the case is closed.

The follow-up report is used by the investigating officer to report progress on the case, additional details, descriptions of new suspects, persons apprehended, property recovered, proposed changes in the classification of the offense report, and any other action taken. The follow-up report may also be used by the officer to indicate that no substantial progress appears possible and that the case should be declared inactive.

If the investigating officer has not submitted the reports as indicated above, the records unit should automatically, through its follow-up control system, note this failure and report the matter to the individual's commanding officer. The case should be kept open on an active basis until the necessary reports are submitted. Only in this manner can a strict control be maintained over case investigation.

BIBLIOGRAPHY

Bristow, Allen P.: *Effective Police Manpower Utilization.* Springfield, Thomas, 1969.

Castellanos, Israel: *Identification Problems.* R. V. Basuino, 1939.

Eastman Kodak Company: *Photography in Law Enforcement.* 1959.

Eldefonso, Edward, Coffey, Alan, and Grace, Richard C.: *Principles of Law Enforcement.* New York, John Wiley, 1967.

Field, Annita T.: *Fingerprint Handbook.* Springfield, Thomas, 1959.

Fricke, Charles W.: *Criminal Investigation.* O. W. Smith, 1930.

Gerber, Samuel R., and Schroeder, Oliver: *Criminal Investigation and Interrogation,* W. H. Anderson Company, 1962.

Harney, Malachi L., and Cross, John C.: *The Informer in Law Enforcement.* Springfield, Thomas, 1960.

Heffron, Floyd N.: *Evidence for the Patrolman.* Springfield, Thomas, 1958.

Leonard, V. A.: *Police Organization and Management,* 2nd ed. Santa Ana, Foundation Press, 1964.

Leonard, V. A.: *The Police, the Judiciary and the Criminal.* Springfield, Thomas, 1969.

Nelson, Alfred T., and Smith, Howard E.: *Car Clouting.* Springfield, Thomas, 1958.

O'Hara, Charles E.: *Fundamentals of Criminal Investigation.* Springfield, Thomas, 1956.

President's Commission on Law Enforcement and Administration of Justice: *The Challenge of Crime in a Free Society; Task Force Report: The Police.* 1967.

Scott, Charles C.: *Photographic Evidence.* Vernon Law Book Company, 1955.

Snyder, LeMoyne: *Homicide Investigation.* Springfield, Thomas, 1949.

Svensson, Arne, Wendel, Otto, and Nicol, Joseph D.: *Techniques of Crime Scene Investigation.* New York, American Elsevier Publishing Company, 1965.

Vanderbosch, Charles G.: *Criminal Investigation.* International Association of Chiefs of Police, 1968.

Wall, Patrick M.: *Eye-Witness Identification in Criminal Cases.* Springfield, Thomas, 1965.

War Department: *Criminal Investigation.* 1945.

Wilson, O. W.: *Police Administration.* New York, McGraw-Hill, 1950.

Wilson, O. W.: *Police Records, Their Installation and Use.* Public Administration Service, 1942.

Wilson, Robert A.: *Homicide Investigation Techniques.* Springfield, Thomas, 1961.

INDEX

109